READING FOR TODAY
THEMES 1

FOURTH EDITION

English Language Programs
Ohio Northern University
525 S. Main Street
Ada, OH 45810

LORRAINE C. SMITH
AND
NANCY NICI MARE

English Language Institute
Queens College
The City University of New York

NATIONAL GEOGRAPHIC LEARNING | CENGAGE Learning

Australia • Brazil • Mexico • Singapore • United Kingdom • United States

Reading for Today 1: Themes
Fourth Edition
Lorraine C. Smith and Nancy Nici Mare

Publisher: Sherrise Roehr

Executive Editor: Laura Le Dréan

Acquisitions Editor: Jennifer Monaghan

Senior Development Editor:
Mary Whittemore

Editorial Assistant: Patricia Giunta

Director of Marketing: Ian Martin

Executive Marketing Manager: Ben Rivera

Product Marketing Manager: Dalia Bravo

Senior Director, Production:
Michael Burggren

Content Production Manager:
Mark Rzeszutek

Senior Print Buyer: Mary Beth Hennebury

Compositor: Lumina Datamatics, Inc.

Cover and Interior Design:
Brenda Carmichael

Cover Photo: Wood abstract of a staircase
constructed piece by piece. Photo
by Roberto Machado Noa.

For permission to use material from this text or product, submit a request online at **www.cengage.com/permissions.** Any additional questions about permissions can be submitted by email to **permissionrequest@cengage.com.**

ISBN-13: 978-1-305-57995-8

National Geographic Learning
20 Channel Center Street
Boston, MA 02210
USA

Cengage Learning is a leading provider of customized learning solutions with office locations around the globe, including Singapore, the United Kingdom, Australia, Mexico, Brazil, and Japan. Locate your local office at **international.cengage.com/region**

Cengage Learning products are represented in Canada by Nelson Education, Ltd.

Visit National Geographic Learning online at **ngl.cengage.com**

Visit our corporate website at **www.cengage.com**

Printed in Canada
Print Number: 01   Print Year: 2015

CONTENTS

SCOPE & SEQUENCE

Unit & Theme	Chapter	Reading Skills	Vocabulary Skills	Critical Thinking Skills
UNIT 1 **New Experiences** Page 2	**CHAPTER 1** Healthy in College Page 4	Previewing a reading Scanning for information Skimming for main idea Predicting content **Reading Skill Focus:** Using headings to create an outline	Understanding meaning from context **Word Forms:** Recognizing the suffix -ful Identifying word forms: adjectives and nouns	Creating a healthy diet Deciding on the best diet Creating a schedule Comparing schedules Discussing questions related to the reading
	CHAPTER 2 Learning a Second Language Page 18	Previewing a reading Activating prior knowledge Scanning for information Predicting content **Reading Skill Focus:** Creating an outline	Understanding meaning from context **Word Forms:** Identifying parts of speech: nouns and verbs	Surveying classmates Evaluating suggestions Comparing lists Categorizing information Discussing opinions
UNIT 2 **Today's Families** Page 32	**CHAPTER 3** A Musical Family Page 34	Previewing a reading Using a chart to answer questions Recalling information Scanning for information **Reading Skill Focus:** Understanding time order words	Understanding meaning from context **Word Forms:** Identifying parts of speech: nouns and verbs	Explaining opinions Proposing changes Recalling information Organizing ideas in a chart Discussing questions related to the reading
	CHAPTER 4 The McCaugheys: An Unusual Family Page 48	Previewing a reading Using a chart to answer questions Predicting content Scanning for information **Reading Skill Focus:** Understanding a bar graph	Understanding meaning from context **Word Forms:** Identifying parts of speech: nouns and verbs	Creating a schedule Discussing opinions Assessing grocery needs Preparing a grocery list Writing questions

SCOPE & SEQUENCE

Unit & Theme	Chapter	Reading Skills	Vocabulary Skills	Critical Thinking Skills
UNIT 3 **Learning and Memory** Page 62	**CHAPTER 5** It's OK to make mistakes! Page 64	Previewing a reading Activating prior knowledge Understanding questions Scanning for information **Reading Skill Focus:** Creating a flowchart	Understanding meaning from context **Word Forms:** Identifying parts of speech: nouns and verbs	Evaluating learning styles Considering real-world applications Explaining preferences Developing a plan Identifying problems
	CHAPTER 6 Super Memory Page 78	Previewing a reading Predicting content Understanding questions Scanning for information **Reading Skill Focus:** Understanding adverbs	Understanding meaning from context **Word Forms:** Identifying parts of speech: adjectives and adverbs	Arguing advantages and disadvantages Identifying reasons Recalling memories Creating a list Comparing lists Discussing questions related to the reading
UNIT 4 **Big Cities and Small Towns** Page 92	**CHAPTER 7** The Best Place to Live Page 94	Activating prior knowledge Previewing a reading Predicting content Scanning for information Skimming for main idea **Reading Skill Focus:** Reading a pie chart	Understanding meaning from context **Word Forms:** Recognizing the suffix *-ness* Identifying parts of speech: adjectives and nouns	Creating a list Assessing reasons Explaining opinions Surveying classmates Comparing charts Discussing questions related to the reading
	CHAPTER 8 The New York City Marathon: A World Race Page 108	Previewing a reading Predicting content Scanning for information Skimming for main idea **Reading Skill Focus:** Understanding a line graph	Understanding meaning from context **Word Forms:** Recognizing the suffix *-ment* Identifying parts of speech: verbs and nouns	Recalling and discussing experiences Comparing advice Writing a letter Describing a sporting event Creating a list Comparing lists

SCOPE & SEQUENCE

Unit & Theme	Chapter	Reading Skills	Vocabulary Skills	Critical Thinking Skills
UNIT 5 **Remarkable Researchers** Page 122	**CHAPTER 9** Margaret Mead: The World Was Her Home Page 124	Previewing a reading Predicting content Scanning for information Skimming for main idea **Reading Skill Focus:** Using a timeline	Understanding meaning from context **Word Forms:** Recognizing the suffixes -ence and -ance Identifying parts of speech: verbs and nouns	Describing an important person Explaining an opinion Evaluating a description Planning an interview Discussing interview results
	CHAPTER 10 Louis Pasteur: A Modern-Day Scientist Page 138	Previewing a reading Activating prior knowledge Predicting content Scanning for information **Reading Skill Focus:** Understanding coordinating conjunctions	Understanding meaning from context **Word Forms:** Recognizing the suffix -tion Identifying parts of speech: verbs and nouns	Recalling experiences Predicting medical advances Identifying past cures Creating a list Comparing lists Evaluating medical discoveries
UNIT 6 **Technology in Our Lives** Page 154	**CHAPTER 11** The Cell Phone Debate Page 156	Previewing a reading Using a chart to record answers Predicting content Scanning for information Skimming for main idea **Reading Skill Focus:** Using a For and Against Chart	Understanding meaning from context **Word Forms:** Recognizing the suffix -ment Identifying parts of speech: verbs and nouns	Considering opposing viewpoints Arguing an opinion Categorizing information Organizing points in a For and Against Chart Debating opposing viewpoints Creating a list of rules
	CHAPTER 12 Clues and Criminal Investigation Page 170	Previewing a reading Using a chart to record ideas Predicting content Scanning for information Skimming for main idea **Reading Skill Focus:** Understanding chronological order	Understanding meaning from context **Word Forms:** Recognizing the suffix -ful Identifying parts of speech: nouns and adjectives	Analyzing evidence Deciding a criminal verdict Discussing opinions Illustrating a criminal investigation Identifying evidence Creating a list Comparing lists Discussing questions related to the reading

PREFACE

Themes for Today, Fourth Edition, is a reading skills text intended for beginning English-as-a-second or foreign-language (ESL/EFL) students. The topics in this text are fresh and timely, and the book has a strong global focus. *Themes for Today* is one in a series of five reading skills texts. The complete series, *Reading for Today,* has been designed to meet the needs of students from the beginning to the advanced levels and includes the following:

- *Reading for Today 1: Themes for Today*   beginning
- *Reading for Today 2: Insights for Today*   high-beginning
- *Reading for Today 3: Issues for Today*   intermediate
- *Reading for Today 4: Concepts for Today*   high-intermediate
- *Reading for Today 5: Topics for Today*   advanced

Themes for Today, Fourth Edition, provides students with essential practice in the types of reading skills they will need in an academic environment. It requires students not only to read text but also to extract basic information from various kinds of charts, graphs, illustrations, maps, and photos. Beginning-level students are rarely exposed to this type of reading material. In addition, they are given the opportunity to speak and write about their own cultures and compare their experiences with those of students from other countries. The text also includes activities that encourage students to go outside the classroom. These tasks provide students with opportunities to practice reading, writing, speaking, and listening to English in the real world. Thus, all four skills are incorporated into each chapter.

Themes for Today, Fourth Edition, has been designed for flexible use by teachers and students. The text consists of six units. Each unit contains two chapters that deal with related topics. At the same time, though, each chapter is entirely separate from the other chapters' content. This gives the instructor the option of either completing entire units or choosing individual chapters as a focus in class. Although the chapters are organized by level of difficulty, the teacher and students may choose to work with the chapters out of order, depending on available time and the interests of the class. The activities and exercises in each chapter have been organized to flow from general comprehension—including main ideas and supporting details—to vocabulary in context, to critical thinking skills. However, the teacher may choose to present the exercises in any order, depending on time and on the students' abilities.

Readers, especially beginning second language readers, vary considerably in their strategy use and comprehension-monitoring activities. Some readers benefit more from focusing on reading one or two paragraphs at a time and checking their comprehension before continuing to read further. Other readers may prefer to read an entire passage and then consider questions related to the reading as a whole. Consequently, in order to provide maximum flexibility, all the reading passages are presented in two formats: (1) in sections and (2) in their complete form. When the reading is presented in sections, each segment is followed by questions on content and vocabulary. Where the reading is presented in its complete form, it is followed by questions on content that ask the reader for inferences, conclusions, opinions, and main ideas. With this dual format, the teacher and students have three choices: All the students may read the passage in segments and then read it in its entirety; all the students may read the passage completely first and then attend to the questions following each segment; or the students may each choose which format they prefer to read first, according to their own preferences and needs.

The exercises that follow the reading passages are carefully crafted to help students develop and improve vocabulary, reading proficiency, and comprehension of English sentence structure.

Lower-level language students need considerable visual reinforcement of ideas and vocabulary. Therefore, this text contains many photos that illustrate the passages' ideas and concepts. In addition, many of the follow-up activities enable students to manipulate the information in the text. The teacher may want the students to use the board to work on the charts and lists in the activities throughout the chapters.

Much of the vocabulary is recycled in the exercises and activities in any given chapter, as well as throughout the book. Experience has shown that beginning-level students especially need repeated exposure to new vocabulary and word forms. Repetition of vocabulary in varied contexts helps the students not only understand the new vocabulary better, but also remember it.

As students work through the text, they will improve their reading skills and develop confidence in their growing English proficiency. At the same time, the teacher will notice the students' steady progress toward skillful, independent reading.

New to the Fourth Edition

The fourth edition of *Themes for Today* maintains the effective approach of the third edition with several significant improvements.

The fourth edition of *Themes for Today* incorporates a number of revisions and new material. Four completely new chapters have been added: *Healthy in College* in Unit 1, *It's OK to make mistakes!* and *Super Memory* in Unit 3, and *The Cell Phone Debate* in Unit 6. All other readings have been revised and updated. The *Vocabulary Skill* exercise has been revised to put the items in the context of the reading, making a clearer connection between the reading passage and the exercise. A new section, *Reading Skill*, focuses on a specific reading skill, for example, understanding graphs and charts, creating flowcharts and timelines, and understanding the meaning of time markers and adverbs that connect two related ideas. Also new to the fourth addition is a *Critical Thinking* section. The activities in this section encourage students to use the information and vocabulary from the passages both orally and in writing, and to think beyond the reading passage and form their own opinions about the topic. In addition, the fourth edition includes new photos, graphs, and charts, all of which are designed to enhance students' comprehension of the readings.

These enhancements to *Themes for Today, Fourth Edition,* have been made to help students improve their reading skills, to reinforce vocabulary, and to encourage interest in the topics. These skills are intended to prepare students for academic work and the technical world of information they will soon encounter.

INTRODUCTION

How to Use This Book

Every chapter in this book consists of the following:

- *Prereading*
- *Reading Passage in Segments with Reading Analysis*
- *Complete Reading Passage*
- *Scanning for Information*
- *Vocabulary Skills*
- *Vocabulary in Context*
- *Reading Skill*
- *Topics for Discussion and Writing*
- *Critical Thinking*
- *Cloze Quiz*
- *Crossword Puzzle*

The format of each chapter in the book is consistent. Although each chapter can be done entirely in class, some exercises may be assigned for homework. This, of course, depends on the individual teacher's preference as well as the availability of class time. Class work will be most effective when done in pairs or groups, giving the students more opportunity to interact with the material and with each other. Each chapter contains the following sections.

Prereading

The *Prereading* section is designed to stimulate student interest and provide preliminary vocabulary for the passage itself. The importance of prereading preparation should not be underestimated. Studies have shown the positive effects of prereading preparation in motivating students and in enhancing reading comprehension. In fact, prereading discussion of topics and visuals has been shown to be more effective in improving reading comprehension than prereading vocabulary exercises. Time should be spent describing and discussing the photos as well as discussing the prereading questions. Furthermore, students should try to relate the topics to their own experience and try to predict what they are going to read about. Students may even choose to write a story based on the chapter-opening photo.

Reading Passage in Segments with Reading Analysis

Each reading passage is presented in segments. As the students read the passage for the first time, they can focus on the meaning of each paragraph. The reading analysis questions that follow each segment require students to think about the meanings of words and phrases, the structure of sentences and paragraphs, the relationships of ideas to each other, and the main idea of the passage. Students also have an opportunity to think about and predict what they will read in the next section of the reading. These exercises are very effective when done in groups. They may also be done individually, but group work gives the students an opportunity to discuss possible answers.

Reading Passage

Students should be instructed to read the entire passage carefully a second time and to pay attention to the main idea and important details.

Scanning for Information

After students have read the complete passage, they read the questions in this exercise, scan the complete passage for the answers, and either indicate the correct answer or write the answer under each question. The last question in this section always refers to the main idea. When students have finished, they may compare their answers with a classmate's. The pairs of students can then refer back to the passage and check their answers. Some students may prefer to work in pairs throughout this exercise.

Vocabulary Skills

The *Vocabulary Skills* sections in this book focus on recognizing and using word forms. In order to successfully complete the *Vocabulary Skill* exercises in this book, the students will need to understand parts of speech, specifically nouns, verbs, adjectives, and adverbs. Teachers should point out the position of each word form in a sentence. Students will develop a sense for which part of speech is necessary in a given sentence. Because this is a low-level text, the *Vocabulary Skill* exercises simply ask students to identify the correct part of speech. They do not need to consider the tense of verbs or the number (singular or plural) of nouns.

Vocabulary in Context

This section consists of a fill-in exercise that is designed as a review of the items in the previous exercises. The vocabulary may have been introduced in the Prereading, or addressed when students read each passage in segments. This exercise may be done for homework as a review or in class as group work.

Reading Skill

Each chapter includes a specific *Reading Skill* section in addition to the *Scanning for Information* section. Each *Reading Skill* section provides instruction and practice with a specific reading skill, such as understanding pie charts, line or bar graphs, or timelines, or creating a flowchart or an outline. These sections also teach students about specific vocabulary or grammar, such as time markers, coordinating conjunctions, or adverbs that help show the connections between sentences. This section is very effective when done in pairs or small groups. The exercises in these sections may also be done individually, but group work gives the students an opportunity to discuss their work.

Topics for Discussion and Writing

This section provides ideas or questions for the students to think about and/or work on alone, in pairs, or in small groups. It provides beginning students with writing opportunities appropriate for their ability level, usually at the paragraph level. In addition, this section includes a *Write in your journal* question that encourages students to respond to a certain aspect of the reading in a personal way.

Critical Thinking

This section contains various activities appropriate to the information in the passages. Some activities are designed for pair and small group work. Students are encouraged to use the information and vocabulary from the passages both orally and in writing. The activities in the *Critical Thinking* section provide students with an opportunity to think about certain aspects of the chapter topic, and to give their own thoughts and opinions about them. The goal of this section is for students to go beyond the reading itself and to form their own ideas and opinions on specific aspects of the topic. Teachers may also use these questions and activities as homework or in-class assignments. The activities in this section help students interact with the real world since many exercises require students to go outside the classroom to collect specific information.

Cloze Quiz

The *Cloze Quiz* is the reading passage itself with 10 to 20 vocabulary items omitted. This section tests not only vocabulary but also sentence structure and comprehension in general. The students are given the words to be written in the blank spaces.

Crossword Puzzle

Each chapter contains a crossword puzzle based on the vocabulary addressed in that chapter. Crossword puzzles are especially effective when the students work in pairs.

Working together provides students with an opportunity to speak together and to discuss their reasons for their answers.

If students need practice pronouncing the letters of the alphabet, they can go over the puzzle orally—the teacher can have the students spell out their answers in addition to pronouncing the words themselves. Students invariably enjoy doing crossword puzzles. They are a fun way to reinforce the vocabulary presented in the various exercises in each chapter, and they require students to pay attention to correct spelling.

Index of Key Words and Phrases

The *Index of Key Words and Phrases* is at the back of the book. This section contains words and phrases from all the chapters for easy reference. This index can help students locate words they need or wish to review. The words that are part of the Academic Word Lists are indicated with an icon.

Skills Index

The *Skills Index* lists the different skills presented and practiced in the book.

ACKNOWLEDGMENTS

The authors and publisher would like to thank the following reviewers:

Sola Armanious, Hudson County Community College; **Marina Broeder**, Mission College; **Kara Chambers**, Mission College; **Peter Chin**, Waseda University International; **Feri Collins**, BIR Training Center; **Courtney DeRouen**, University of Washington; **Jeanne de Simon**, University of West Florida; **Shoshana Dworkin**, BIR Training Center; **Cindy Etter**, University of Washington International and English Language Programs; **Ken Fackler**, University of Tennessee at Martin; **Jan Hinson**, Carson Newman University; **Chigusa Katoku**, Mission College; **Sharon Kruzic**, Mission College; **Carmella Lieskle**, Shimane University; **Yelena Malchenko**, BIR Training Center; **Mercedes Mont**, Miami Dade College; **Ewa Paluch**, BIR Training Center; **Barbara Pijan**, Portland State University, Intensive English Language Program; **Julaine Rosner**, Mission College; **Julie Scales**, University of Washington; **Mike Sfiropoulos**, Palm Beach State College; **Barbara Smith-Palinkas**, Hillsborough Community College; **Eileen Sotak**, BIR Training Center; **Matthew Watterson**, Hongik University; **Tristinn Williams**, IELP—University of Washington; **Iryna Zhylina**, Hudson County Community College; **Ana Zuljevic**, BIR Training Center.

From the Authors:
We are thankful to everyone at National Geographic Learning, especially Laura LeDréan, Mary Whittemore, Patricia Giunta, and Jennifer Monaghan, for their unwavering support. We are extremely grateful to all the teachers and students who use our book, and who never hesitate to give us such incredible feedback. As always, we are very appreciative of the ongoing encouragement from our families, friends, and colleagues.

Dedication:
To Tom

New Experiences

A tourist in Shanghai eats scorpions on a stick.

1. How do you feel when you have new experiences?

2. How can new experiences be good for us?

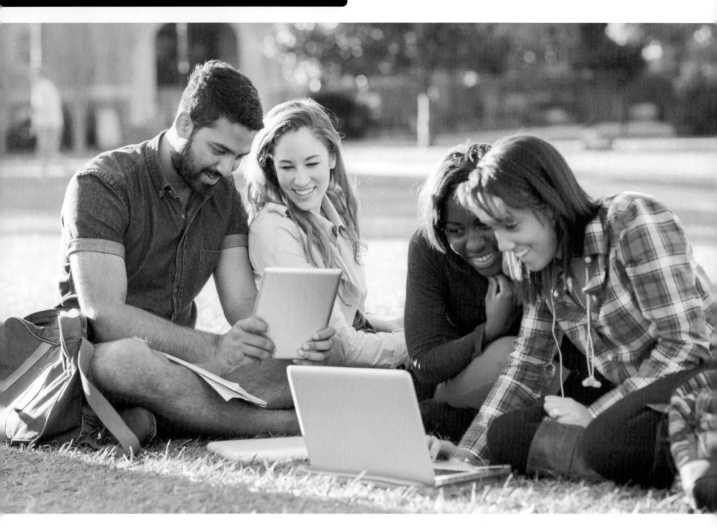

Prereading

1. Look at the photo. What are these students doing? Are they happy or unhappy? Why do you think so?

2. Read the title of this chapter. What will you read about?
   a. How to find a good college
   b. How to get good grades in college
   c. How to have a good life at college

3. Work with two or three classmates. What are some ways to have a healthy life while you are in college? Compare your ideas with your classmates' ideas.

Reading

Read each paragraph carefully. Then answer the questions.

Healthy in College

It is your first year at a college or university. Of course, you are very excited. You are away from your home for the first time. The college campus is beautiful. Everyone is very helpful. At the same time, nothing is familiar to you. Everything is different. You feel some stress. It's important to take care of yourself. How can you stay healthy?

1. **Of course**, you are very excited.
    a. **Of course** means
        1. maybe.
        2. always.
        3. naturally.
    b. You are excited because
        1. it is your first year of college.
        2. the college is beautiful.
        3. you have many new classes.

2. The college **campus** is
    a. the area and buildings of a college.
    b. the trees and flowers of a college.
    c. the neighborhood around a college.

3. **Nothing** is familiar to you. **Everything** is different.
    a. **Nothing** and **everything** have
        1. opposite meanings.
        2. the same meaning.
    b. **Familiar** means
        1. different.
        2. the same.
        3. new.
    c. **Nothing is familiar to you** because
        1. you are excited.
        2. everything is new to you.
        3. the campus is beautiful.

4. **Stress** means
    a. happiness.
    b. worry.
    c. sickness.

5. **Stay healthy** means
    a. keep in good health.
    b. become sick.
    c. be successful in college.

6. What do you think the next paragraph will discuss?
    a. Your college
    b. Your new classes
    c. Your health

Eat a Healthy Diet

You usually eat when you are hungry, but sometimes you eat when you are not really hungry. Instead, you may be thirsty! It is a good idea to drink often. Water is the best choice. Green tea is an excellent choice, too. You should stay away from sweet fruit juices and soft drinks, such as soda. These are not healthy beverages.

7. Your **diet** is
    a. the food you always eat.
    b. the food you eat when you are hungry.
    c. the food you eat that is healthy.

8. You are **thirsty**. You need
    a. some food.
    b. a drink.
    c. to sleep.

9. **The best choice** means a good
    a. decision.
    b. drink.
    c. place.

10. You should stay away from sweet fruit juices and soft drinks, such as soda.
    a. This sentence means
        1. you can drink sweet fruit juices and soft drinks.
        2. don't drink sweet fruit juices and soft drinks.
    b. **Such as** means
        1. for example.
        2. except.
        3. also.

11. _____ True _____ False   The best drinks are water and green tea.

12. **Beverages** are
    a. kinds of food.
    b. kinds of fruit.
    c. kinds of drinks.

When you are hungry, eat fresh food and produce, such as fruit and vegetables. These are nutritious. Don't eat a lot of junk food because it has a lot of fat and sugar. This kind of food isn't nutritious. Junk food is not a healthy snack.

13. What is **produce**?
    a. Fat and sugar
    b. Fruit and vegetables
    c. Junk food

14. _____ True _____ False   **Nutritious** food is good for your health.

15. **This kind** of food isn't nutritious.
    a. **This kind** means
        1. fruit and vegetables.
        2. fresh food.
        3. junk food.
    b. **Kind** means
        1. type.
        2. food.
        3. drink.

16. Don't eat junk food because
    a. it isn't nutritious.
    b. it is expensive.
    c. it is healthy.

17. A **snack** is
    a. a meal.
    b. a drink.
    c. a little food.

Get Enough Rest

   Most college students do not get enough sleep. They have a lot of homework, and they have to study for exams. In addition, most students take a lot of classes every semester, but they want to socialize, too. They like to go out in the evening with friends, or play sports after classes. They usually stay up very late every night. But most people need seven or eight hours of sleep at night. It is important to get enough sleep. Try to take a nap during the day. Sometimes a twenty-minute nap in a quiet place can be very restful.

18. **Most college students do not get enough sleep** means
    a. they sleep too little.
    b. they sleep too much.
    c. they never sleep.

19. **In addition** means
    a. after.
    b. but.
    c. also.

20. Students **socialize** when they
    a. spend time with friends.
    b. do their homework alone.
    c. take a lot of classes.

21. **Stay up late** means
    a. go to bed very late.
    b. go to bed very early.
    c. study all night.

22. **Take a nap** means to sleep
    a. a long time.
    b. a short time.
    c. in the library.

23. A nap is **restful** because
   a. it makes you feel awake.
   b. it helps you study.
   c. it makes you tired.

Conclusion

Eat well, drink a lot of water, and get enough rest. When you are healthy, you feel happy. When you feel good, you can pay attention in class, study hard, and do well on your exams. You will be a successful college student!

---

24. Get enough **rest** means
   a. eat a lot of food.
   b. sleep the right number of hours.
   c. don't get sick.

CD 1
TR 2
Read the complete passage. Then answer the questions that follow.

Healthy in College

1   It is your first year at a college or university. Of course, you are very excited. You
2   are away from your home for the first time. The college campus is beautiful. Everyone
3   is very helpful. At the same time, nothing is familiar to you. Everything is different.
4   You feel some stress. It's important to take care of yourself. How can you stay
5   healthy?

Eat a Healthy Diet

6   You usually eat when you are hungry, but sometimes you eat when you are not
7   really hungry. Instead, you may be thirsty! It is a good idea to drink often. Water is
8   the best choice. Green tea is an excellent choice, too. You should stay away from sweet
9   fruit juices and soft drinks, such as soda. These are not healthy beverages.
10 When you are hungry, eat fresh food and produce, such as fruit and vegetables.
11 These are nutritious. Don't eat a lot of junk food because it has a lot of fat and sugar.
12 This kind of food isn't nutritious. Junk food is not a healthy snack.

Get Enough Rest

Most college students do not get enough sleep. They have a lot of homework, and they have to study for exams. In addition, most students take a lot of classes every semester, but they want to socialize, too. They like to go out in the evening with friends, or play sports after classes. They usually stay up very late every night. But most people need seven or eight hours of sleep at night. It is important to get enough sleep. Try to take a nap during the day. Sometimes a twenty-minute nap in a quiet place can be very restful.

Conclusion

Eat well, drink a lot of water, and get enough rest. When you are healthy, you feel happy. When you feel good, you can pay attention in class, study hard, and do well on your exams. You will be a successful college student!

Scanning for Information

Read the questions. Then go back to the complete passage and scan quickly for the answers. Check (√) or circle the letter of the correct answers.

1. What are some reasons to be happy in your first year at college?
   Check (√) all that apply.
   a. _____ The college campus is beautiful.
   b. _____ You do not know anyone.
   c. _____ You are in college now.
   d. _____ Everyone is helpful.
   e. _____ The campus is strange to you.

2. Why do some students feel stress in their first year at college? Check (√) all that apply.
   a. _____ They do not know any other students.
   b. _____ Everyone seems friendly.
   c. _____ They have a lot of classes and homework.
   d. _____ Nothing is familiar to them.
   e. _____ The campus is a beautiful place.

3. Why do we sometimes eat when we are not hungry?
   a. Because we are really thirsty
   b. Because we are excited
   c. Because someone buys us food

4. Why is it a bad idea to eat junk food?
   a. Because junk food is expensive
   b. Because junk food makes us feel stress
   c. Because junk food is not healthy

5. Why don't most college students get enough sleep?
   a. They have to do homework and study for tests.
   b. They are away from home.
   c. They take a nap during the day.

6. What is the main idea of the story?
   a. College is exciting.
   b. Junk food is not healthy.
   c. It is important to stay healthy in college.

Vocabulary Skill

Recognizing Word Forms

In English, some nouns become adjectives by adding the suffix *–ful*, for example, *use* (n.), *useful* (adj.).

Read the sentences below. Decide if the correct word is a noun or an adjective. Circle your answer. Do the examples below as a class before you begin.

> **EXAMPLES:**
>
> a. ID cards are <u>use / useful</u> for new students.
>   (n.)   (adj.)
>
> b. My ID card has many <u>uses / useful</u>. I buy food and books with it.
>   (n.)   (adj.)

1. Our new college professor is very <u>help / helpful</u>.
      (n.)   (adj.)

2. His <u>help / helpful</u> is important to us.
      (n.)   (adj.)

3. Students enjoy the <u>beauty / beautiful</u> of the new campus.
      (n.)   (adj.)

4. This is a <u>beauty / beautiful</u> college.
      (n.)   (adj.)

5. It can be very <u>stress / stressful</u> to go to a new college or university.
      (n.)   (adj.)

6. Luke feels a lot of <u>stress / stressful</u> because he has a lot of homework every night.
      (n.)   (adj.)

7. Fruit and vegetables are good for your <u>health / healthful</u>.
      (n.)   (adj.)

8. Junk food is not very <u>health / healthful</u>.
      (n.)   (adj.)

9. Emily always gets enough <u>rest / restful</u> before a big test.
      (n.)   (adj.)

10. A short nap can be very <u>rest / restful</u>.
      (n.)   (adj.)

Vocabulary in Context

Read the following sentences. Choose the correct word or phrase for each sentence.
Fill in the blanks.

campus (n.)	in addition	thirsty (adj.)

1. I am very _____. May I have some water?

2. This college has a very small _____. There are not many buildings.

3. Lucas plays the piano. _____, he plays the violin and the drums.

familiar (adj.)	of course	socialize (v.)

4. Claire likes to _____ with her friends after class. They sometimes go to the movies together.

5. Tom worked ten hours today. _____, he is very tired!

6. I am _____ with this campus. I can help you find the bookstore.

choice (n.)	healthy (adj.)	stress (n.)	such as

7. Susan enjoys many kinds of fruit, _____ apples, pears, and bananas.

8. My parents are very _____. They eat well and exercise every day.

9. Steven has a lot of _____. He is always worried about his work.

10. Eggs are a good _____ for breakfast. They cook very quickly.

Reading Skill

Using Headings to Create an Outline

Readings often include headings. Headings introduce new ideas or topics. They also introduce details. Using headings to make an outline can help you understand and remember the most important information from a reading passage.

Read the passage again. Use these sentences to complete the outline below.

- Don't eat junk food.
- Eat well, drink a lot of water, and get enough rest.
- You feel some stress.
- Try to take a nap during the day.
- It's important to take care of yourself.
- Get enough rest.
- Eat fresh food and produce.

Healthy in College

I. <u>Introduction</u>
    A. *The campus is beautiful, and everyone is helpful.*

    B.

    C.

II. <u>Eat a Healthy Diet</u>
    A. *It is a good idea to drink often. Water is the best choice.*

    B.

    C.

III. _____
    A. *Students need at least seven or eight hours of sleep every night.*

    B.

IV. *Conclusion*
    A.

    B. *You will be a successful college student.*

Topics for Discussion and Writing

1. Many college students play sports after school. Is this a good idea? Why or why not?

2. What are some other ways students can be healthy in college? Make a list.

3. Write in your journal. Do you like to study alone or with your friends? Why?

Critical Thinking

1. Work with three or four classmates. Create a healthy diet for one week for a busy college student. When you are finished, compare your diet with other groups' diets. Decide on the best diet.

2. Work with three or four classmates. Create a schedule for a busy college student. Be sure to include time for rest. When you are finished, compare your schedule with other groups' schedules. Decide on the best one, or create a single class schedule.

3. Is it easy to be healthy in college? Why or why not? Discuss these questions with a partner.

Cloze Quiz

Read the following passage. Fill in the blanks with the correct words from the list. Use each word or phrase only once.

beverages	choice	hungry	such as	thirsty

You usually eat when you are _____(1)_____, but sometimes you eat when you are not really hungry. Instead, you may be _____(2)_____! It is a good idea to drink often. Water is the best _____(3)_____. Green tea is an excellent choice, too. You should stay away from sweet fruit juices and soft drinks, _____(4)_____ soda. These are not healthy _____(5)_____.

junk	kind	nutritious	produce	snack

When you are hungry, eat fresh food and _____(6)_____, such as fruit and vegetables. These are nutritious. Don't eat a lot of _____(7)_____ food because it has a lot of fat and sugar. This _____(8)_____ of food isn't _____(9)_____. Junk food is not a healthy _____(10)_____.

Crossword Puzzle

Review the words in the box below. Then read the clues on the next page. Write the words in the correct spaces in the puzzle.

beverage	familiar	nap	snack
campus	healthy	nothing	socialize
choice	hungry	produce	stress
diet	kind	rest	thirsty

Crossword Puzzle Clues

ACROSS CLUES

2. I have a _____ of colleges to go to. I need to decide.

4. What _____ of vegetable is this? It looks like broccoli.

7. I am _____. I need some water.

10. The college _____ has many trees, flowers, and buildings.

12. Most big cities feel _____ to me because I come from a large city.

13. Are you _____? If so, let's get some lunch!

15. A _____ is a drink, such as soda or juice.

16. We won't stay _____ if we do not exercise regularly and eat good food.

DOWN CLUES

1. My _____ is mostly fruit, vegetables, and rice. I do not eat much meat.

3. I feel a lot of _____ just before an exam. I can't relax.

5. I have _____ to do this afternoon. I am free. Do you want to go for a walk with me?

6. After class, I like to _____ with my friends.

8. Susan looks tired. She needs to get some _____.

9. Candy is not a good _____. It has a lot of sugar. Eat a piece of fruit instead.

11. You can buy fresh _____, such as fruit and vegetables, at the local market.

14. John tries to take a 30-minute _____ every afternoon. This short sleep gives him energy.

Students have class in a language lab.

Prereading

1. Read the title of this chapter. What will you read about?

    a. I will read about different languages I can learn.

    b. I will read about ways to learn another language.

    c. I will read about a second language that is different from my language.

2. Work with a partner. How can you learn a second language? Make a list of things you can do in the chart.

How can you learn a second language?
1.
2.
3.
4.
5.

3. Compare your list with your classmates' lists. Can you add any ideas to your list? Write them here.

_____

_____

_____

Reading

Read each paragraph carefully. Then answer the questions.

Learning a Second Language

Some people learn a second language easily. Other people have trouble learning a new language. How can you help yourself learn a new language, such as English? There are several ways to help you learn English more easily. It can be more interesting, too.

1. _____ True _____ False   Everyone learns a second language easily.

2. Other people have **trouble** learning a new language.
Trouble means
a. difficulty.
b. classes.
c. reasons.

3. There are **several** ways to make learning English a little easier and more interesting.
Several means
a. easier.
b. many.
c. fun.

4. What do you think the next paragraph will discuss?
a. Problems learning a new language
b. Ways to learn a new language more easily
c. Where to study a second language

The first step is to feel positive about learning English. If you believe that you can learn, you will learn. Be patient. You do not have to understand everything all at once. Sometimes you make mistakes when you learn something new. We can learn from our mistakes. In other words, do not worry about mistakes.

5. When we make a **mistake**, we
   a. do something quickly.
   b. do something well.
   c. do something incorrectly.

6. What does it mean to feel **positive** about learning English?
   a. If you believe you can learn, you will learn.
   b. You can understand everything all at once.
   c. You have to make mistakes.

7. When you are **patient**, do you worry about learning English very quickly?
   a. Yes
   b. No

8. You do not have to understand everything **all at once**.
   All at once means
   a. slowly.
   b. easily.
   c. at the same time.

9. We can learn from our mistakes. **In other words**, do not worry about mistakes.
   What follows **in other words**?
   a. An opposite idea
   b. An example
   c. The same idea

10. What do you think the next paragraph will discuss?
    a. Different kinds of languages
    b. Making mistakes
    c. The second step

The second step is to practice your English. For example, you can write in a journal, or diary, every day. Then you will feel comfortable writing your ideas in English. After several weeks, your writing will improve. In addition, you must speak English every day. You can practice with your classmates outside class. You might make mistakes, but it's OK. Gradually you will feel more comfortable when you write and speak in English.

11. What is a **journal**?
   a. A diary
   b. A practice
   c. An example

12. How can you practice your English?
   a. Write in a journal every day.
   b. Practice with your classmates after class.
   c. Both a and b

13. **After several weeks** means
   a. after a few days.
   b. when a few weeks are finished.
   c. a week later.

14. **In addition**, you must speak English every day. What follows **in addition**?
   a. More information
   b. The same information
   c. The result

15. **Gradually** means
   a. quickly.
   b. carefully.
   c. slowly.

16. What do you think the next paragraph will discuss?
   a. Making mistakes
   b. Feeling comfortable
   c. The third step

The third step is to keep a record of your language learning. You can write this in your journal. After each class, think about it. Do you answer questions correctly in class? Do you understand the teacher? Perhaps the lesson is difficult, but you can try to understand it. Write these accomplishments in your journal.

17. When you **keep a record** of something,
    a. you write it on paper.
    b. you remember it.
    c. you tell someone.

18. _____ True _____ False   You can keep a record of your language learning in your journal.

19. **Perhaps** means
    a. usually.
    b. sometimes.
    c. maybe.

20. Write these **accomplishments** in your journal.
    Accomplishments are
    a. successes.
    b. mistakes.
    c. lessons.

You must be positive about learning English. You must believe that you can do it. It is important to practice every day. You can make a record of your achievements. You can enjoy learning English, and you can have more confidence in yourself.

21. **Achievements** are
    a. accomplishments.
    b. lessons.
    c. problems.

22. Read the following actions. Which actions are accomplishments? Circle all correct answers.
    a. You ask a question in class.
    b. You bring a notebook and a pen to class.
    c. You make a mistake, but you understand it.
    d. You try to answer a question in class.
    e. You speak your native language to a classmate.

23. When you have **confidence** in yourself,

    a. you try hard and you never make a mistake.

    b. you believe that you can do something.

    c. you talk about your accomplishments all the time.

 Read the complete passage. Then answer the questions that follow.

CD 1
TR 3

Learning a Second Language

1   Some people learn a second language easily. Other people have trouble learning
2 a new language. How can you help yourself learn a new language, such as English?
3 There are several ways to help you learn English more easily. It can be more
4 interesting, too.
5   The first step is to feel positive about learning English. If you believe that you can
6 learn, you will learn. Be patient. You do not have to understand everything all at once.
7 Sometimes you make mistakes when you learn something new. We can learn from our
8 mistakes. In other words, do not worry about mistakes.
9   The second step is to practice your English. For example, you can write in a journal,
10 or diary, every day. Then you will feel comfortable writing your ideas in English.
11 After several weeks, your writing will improve. In addition, you must speak English
12 every day. You can practice with your classmates outside class. You might make
13 mistakes, but it's OK. Gradually you can feel comfortable when you write and speak
14 in English.

15   The third step is to keep a record of your language learning. You can write this in
16 your journal. After each class, think about it. Do you answer questions correctly in
17 class? Do you understand the teacher? Perhaps the lesson is difficult, but you can try
18 to understand it. Write these accomplishments in your journal.
19   You must be positive about learning English. You must believe that you can do it. It
20 is important to practice every day. You can make a record of your achievements. You
21 can enjoy learning English, and you can have more confidence in yourself.

Scanning for Information

Read the questions. Then go back to the complete passage and scan quickly for the answers. Circle the letter of the correct answer or write your answer in the space provided.

1. Are there ways to make learning a second language easier?
   a. Yes
   b. No

2. How many steps are there? _____

3. What are the steps?

   _____

   _____

   _____

4. What is the main idea of this story?
   a. It is very important to learn a second language.
   b. Some people learn a second language easily. Other people do not.
   c. There are ways to help you learn a second language more easily.

Vocabulary Skill

Recognizing Word Forms

In English, some words can be either a noun (*n.*) or a verb (*v.*), for example, *help*.

Read the sentences below. Decide if the correct word is a noun or a verb. Circle your answer. Do the examples below as a class before you begin.

EXAMPLES:

a. The teacher <u>helps / helps</u> me learn English.
      (v.)   *(n.)*

b. This <u>help / help</u> is very important to me.
      (v.)   *(n.)*

1. When my homework <u>troubles / troubles</u> me, I ask my teacher for help.
                  (v.)   *(n.)*

2. Some people have <u>trouble / trouble</u> when they learn a new language.
                  (v.)   *(n.)*

3. I often make <u>mistakes / mistakes</u> in class.
                         (v.)   *(n.)*

4. I sometimes <u>mistake / mistake</u> the words *there* and *their* when I write.
                          (v.)   *(n.)*

5. The students know the correct <u>answer / answer</u>.
                                 (v.)   *(n.)*

6. We always <u>answer / answer</u> the questions in class.
                    (v.)   *(n.)*

7. After class I <u>practice / practice</u> English with my classmates.
                    (v.)   *(n.)*

8. This <u>practice / practice</u> helps me to learn English.
          (v.)   *(n.)*

Vocabulary in Context

Read the following sentences. Choose the correct word or phrase for each sentence. Fill in the blanks.

all at once	patient *(adj.)*	several *(adj.)*

1. My friends come from many different countries. They also speak
_____ languages.

2. It takes a lot of time to learn a new language. You can't learn everything
_____.

3. My mother is a very _____ person. She works carefully and is never in a hurry to finish anything.

gradually *(adv.)*	in other words	positive *(adj.)*

4. Clark plays the violin every day for two hours. He is _____ improving.

5. I have an English test tomorrow. I always study hard, so I feel very _____ about the test.

6. Lucy eats fresh fruit and vegetables every day. She exercises five times a week, and she sleeps eight hours a night. _____, Lucy has a very healthy life.

| confidence (n.) | in addition | perhaps (adv.) | trouble (n.) |

7. John is very tired today. _____ he didn't sleep well last night.

8. I have _____ with spelling in English. It's very difficult for me.

9. Tony needs to have more _____. He is always afraid to try something new.

10. Pedro practices English with his classmates. _____, he writes in his journal every day.

Reading Skill

Creating an Outline

Outlines list the most important information from a reading. Outlines include information such as headings, details, and examples. Creating an outline can help you understand and remember what you read.

Read the passage again. Write the information in the outline below.

Steps to Help You Learn a Second Language

I. First Step: _____

Example: _____

II. Second Step: _____

Example: _____

III. Third Step: _____

Example: _____

Topics for Discussion and Writing

1. Imagine that you have a friend who plans to come to the United States to study English. Write a letter to your friend. Tell your friend what to expect. Give your friend advice about learning English more easily.

2. When do you use English the most? Where? Write about this and give examples.

3. Where do you prefer to study (for example, at home, in the library)? Why? Talk about this with your classmates.

4. Write in your journal. Make a special place in your journal for your language learning. Write in it several times a week. Do you think your English is improving? Why? Write about your language learning accomplishments.

Critical Thinking

1. What is the most difficult part of learning English for you? Talk to several of your classmates. Ask them for suggestions to help you. Talk to several people outside your class. Ask them for suggestions, too. Try some of these suggestions and then report back to your classmates. Tell them which suggestions were the most helpful and explain why.

2. Look at your lists of things you can do to learn a language on pages 18–19. Work with a partner. Compare and discuss your lists. Where can you do these activities? Which language skills does each activity help you develop? Write them in the chart below. There is an example to help you.

Activity	Language Skills (listening, speaking, reading, writing)	Where can you do this activity?
I ask questions when I don't understand.	speaking and listening	in class, in stores, on the street, at a train station or a bus stop, on the telephone

3. When is the best time to learn a new language? When a person is very young, or in college? Why? Discuss these questions with a partner.

Cloze Quiz

Read the following passage. Fill in the blanks with the correct words from the list. Use each word or phrase only once.

easily	interesting	learn	such as	trouble

Some people learn a second language _____ (1). Other people have _____ (2) learning a new language. How can you help yourself _____ (3) a new language, _____ (4) English?

There are several ways to help you learn English more easily. It can be more _____ (5), too.

achievements	believe	confidence	positive	practice

You must be _____ (6) about learning English. You must _____ (7) that you can do it. It is important to _____ (8) every day. You can make a record of your _____ (9). You will enjoy learning English, and you will have more _____ (10) in yourself.

Crossword Puzzle

Review the words in the box below. Then read the clues on the next page. Write the words in the correct spaces in the puzzle.

accomplishments	learn	perhaps	several
confidence	mistake	positive	steps
gradually	patient	record	trouble
journal			

Crossword Puzzle Clues

ACROSS CLUES

2. When you write something down, you make a _____ of it.

5. Your _____, or achievements, will help you feel more comfortable.

7. When you study English, be _____ because learning another language takes time.

8. A _____ is a diary.

9. You need to feel very _____ about learning English. You need to say, "I can do it!"

11. Anna has _____ remembering new words. This is difficult for her.

12. _____ means slowly; after a long time.

13. It takes time to _____ a second language.

DOWN CLUES

1. If learning English worries you, _____ you need to find ways to worry less.

3. Keep a diary and write your language learning achievements in it. This will give you _____.

4. When we make a _____, we do something incorrectly.

6. I know many _____, or ways, to learn another language.

10. There are _____ ways to learn another language. You already know some of them.

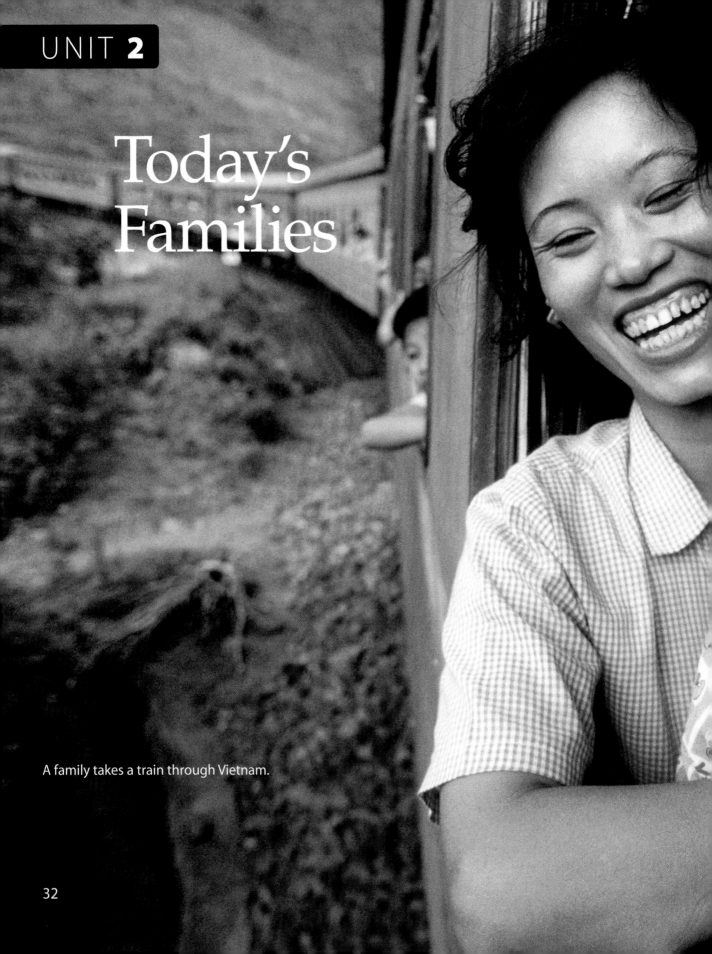

Today's Families

A family takes a train through Vietnam.

1. What are today's families like? How are today's families different from families in the past?

2. Do you know any unusual families? How are they unusual?

Prereading

Look at the photo. Read the title of the story. Then answer the questions.

1. What is the boy doing? _____

2. Where is he doing this?
   a. at school
   b. at home
   c. at a concert

3. How old do you think he is? _____

4. Read the title of the story again. What do you think you will read about? Talk about this with your classmates.

Reading

Read each paragraph carefully. Then answer the questions.

A Musical Family

The Family's City Life

Shawn Cabey and Whitney Gray live with their four children in the city of Chicago, Illinois, in the United States. Every night, the family eats dinner together. Most of the time, the children talk about video games. The oldest child, Nick, does not like to talk about school. He is not doing well in math. Shawn and Whitney are very unhappy. They do not want this life for their children. Soon, they decide to make a change. What do they do?

1. Where does this family live? _____

2. Who are Shawn and Whitney?
   a. The parents
   b. The children

3. _____ True _____ False   The family plays video games together every night.

4. _____ True _____ False   The family eats dinner together every night.

5. What do the children talk about at dinner?
   _____

6. Does Nick like to talk about school? _____

7. **Nick is not doing well in math** means
   a. he does not like math.
   b. he does not get good grades in math.
   c. he does good work in math.

8. Why are Shawn and Whitney unhappy?
   a. They do not like to eat dinner together.
   b. They do not like to talk about video games.
   c. They do not like this life for the family.

9. Soon, they decide to make a change.

    a. **Soon** means

        1. unhappily.

        2. after a short time.

        3. together.

    b. **Decide** means

        1. begin.

        2. want.

        3. make a choice.

10. What do you think the next paragraph will discuss?

    a. The changes that the family makes

    b. The video games that the children play

    c. The unhappy life the family has

Big Changes in the Family's Life

First, Shawn and Whitney decide to sell their house in Chicago. Then, they throw away the video games and move a thousand miles away to a very small town in Maine, in the United States. Next, Whitney decides to "homeschool" the children. This means that she teaches the children at home. After that, Nick begins to enjoy math. Soon, his schoolwork improves, and the other children's schoolwork does, too.

---

11. They **move** a thousand miles away to a very small town in Maine. **Move** means

    a. to change where you live.

    b. to make a long trip.

    c. to decide to do something.

12. They **throw away** the video games. **Throw away** means

    a. give to someone else.

    b. put in the garbage.

    c. sell to someone else.

13. Who is the children's teacher? _____

14. Homeschool means

    a. children go to school near their home.

    b. children do not do homework.

    c. children do not go to school. They learn at home.

15. Why does Whitney decide to homeschool the children?

    a. She wants to help them do better.

    b. She doesn't like their teacher.

    c. The school is 1,000 miles away.

16. Nick begins to **enjoy** math.
    Enjoy means
    a. do.
    b. work.
    c. like.

17. His schoolwork **improves**, and the other children's schoolwork does, too.
    Improve means
    a. become harder.
    b. become better.
    c. become enjoyable.

18. _____ True _____ False   All the children's schoolwork improves.

Family Music Lessons

All the children enjoy their new lives, but sometimes they are bored. Shawn decides to give them music lessons. Now every afternoon, they play their music together. Each child plays a different musical instrument. Nick is 16 years old. He plays the viola. Zack, who is 13 years old, plays the cello. Twelve-year-old Bryanna, the only daughter in the family, plays the violin. The youngest child in the family is Noah. He is only six years old, but he plays the piano very well. In fact, he plays it better than his father! The children love to perform together, and Shawn and Whitney love to listen to them. Now the Gray-Cabey family has a very different life. The town is quiet, but the Gray-Cabey house is noisy!

The Gray-Cabeys Today

The children are adults now, but music and education are still important to this family. Noah, the youngest Gray-Cabey child, is a musician and a TV actor. He is also a college student at Harvard University. Shawn and Whitney are successful parents!

19. All the children enjoy their new lives, but sometimes they are **bored**.
    Bored means
    a. they have a lot of schoolwork to do.
    b. they do not have a lot of interesting things to do.
    c. they do not have a lot of friends.

20. Why does Shawn give them music lessons?
    a. The parents love to listen to the children.
    b. The children don't enjoy their new lives.
    c. The children are bored.

21. Who is the oldest child? _____

22. Who is the youngest child? _____

23. How many daughters do Shawn and Whitney have? _____

24. **The children love to perform together** means
    a. the children love to play music together.
    b. the children love to study together.
    c. the children love to eat dinner together.

25. The Gray-Cabey house is **noisy**. **Noisy** means
    a. full of people.
    b. full of sounds.
    c. very quiet.

26. Why isn't the Gray-Cabey house quiet?
    a. Because the children play video games all day
    b. Because the children study hard at night
    c. Because the children play musical instruments together

27. Why are Shawn and Whitney successful parents?
    a. Because their children are adults now
    b. Because their children still love music and education
    c. Because Noah is a college student

CD 1
TR 4

Read the complete passage. Then answer the questions that follow.

A Musical Family

The Family's City Life

1   Shawn Cabey and Whitney Gray live with their four children in the city of Chicago,
2 Illinois, in the United States. Every night, the family eats dinner together. Most of the
3 time, the children talk about video games. The oldest child, Nick, does not like to talk
4 about school. He is not doing well in math. Shawn and Whitney are very unhappy.
5 They do not want this life for their children. Soon, they decide to make a change.
6 What do they do?

Big Changes in the Family's Life

7   First, Shawn and Whitney decide to sell their house in Chicago. Then, they throw
8 away the video games and move a thousand miles away to a very small town in
9 Maine, in the United States. Next, Whitney decides to "homeschool" the children.
10 This means that she teaches them at home. After that, Nick begins to enjoy math.
11 Soon, his schoolwork improves, and the other children's schoolwork does, too.

Family Music Lessons

12   All the children enjoy their new lives, but sometimes they are bored. Shawn decides
13 to give them music lessons. Now every afternoon, they play their music together.
14 Each child plays a different musical instrument. Nick is 16 years old. He plays the
15 viola. Zack, who is 13 years old, plays the cello. Twelve-year-old Bryanna, the only
16 daughter in the family, plays the violin. The youngest child in the family is Noah. He
17 is only six years old, but he plays the piano very well. In fact, he plays it better than
18 his father! The children love to perform together, and Shawn and Whitney love to
19 listen to them. Now the Gray-Cabey family has a very different life. The town is quiet,
20 but the Gray-Cabey house is noisy!

The Gray-Cabeys Today

21   The children are adults now, but music and education are still important to this
22 family. Noah, the youngest Gray-Cabey, is a musician and a TV actor. He is also a
23 college student at Harvard University.

Noah Gray-Cabey
and his parents at a
television festival

39

Scanning for Information

Read the questions. Then go back to the complete passage and scan quickly for the answers. Check (√) or circle the letter of the correct answers.

1. Why does the Gray-Cabey family move from Chicago to Maine?
   a. They want to live in a small town.
   b. Chicago is not a safe place.
   c. Maine has better schools.

2. What changes does the Gray-Cabey family make? Check (√) all that apply.
   a. _____ They move to a different state.
   b. _____ They stop talking about school.
   c. _____ They throw away the children's video games.
   d. _____ They teach the children at home.
   e. _____ They throw away their TV.
   f. _____ They learn to play musical instruments.

3. All the children enjoy their new lives, but sometimes they are **bored**. Shawn decides to give them music lessons.

   Why are the children bored?

   _____

4. How is the Gray-Cabey family's life different in Maine? Check (√) all that apply.
   a. _____ The children's schoolwork improves.
   b. _____ They play new video games.
   c. _____ They eat dinner together.
   d. _____ Whitney is the children's teacher.
   e. _____ All of the children play musical instruments.
   f. _____ They live in a big city.

5. What is the main idea of this story?
   a. The Gray-Cabey children love to perform music together.
   b. The Gray-Cabey parents want to give their family a better life.
   c. The Gray-Cabey children's schoolwork improves a lot in Maine.

Vocabulary Skill

Recognizing Word Forms

In English, some words can be either a noun (*n.*) or a verb (*v.*), for example, *work*.

Read the sentences below. Decide if the correct word is a noun or a verb. Circle your answer. Do the examples below as a class before you begin.

EXAMPLES:

a. Noah <u>practices / practices</u> the piano every day.
        (v.)   *(n.)*

b. This <u>practice / practice</u> helps him to improve very fast.
     (v.)   *(n.)*

1. Shawn and Whitney <u>move / move</u> to Maine with their family.
      (v.)   *(n.)*

2. They are very happy about the <u>move / move</u>.
       (v.)   *(n.)*

3. Shawn and Whitney <u>love / love</u> their children very much.
     (v.)   *(n.)*

4. The children have a good life because of their parents' <u>love / love</u>.
      (v.)   *(n.)*

5. The Gray-Cabey family decides to <u>change / change</u> their life.
      (v.)   *(n.)*

6. The <u>change / change</u> is very helpful to the family.
    (v.)   *(n.)*

7. Shawn and Whitney have a lot of <u>work / work</u> to do today.
      (v.)   *(n.)*

8. They sometimes <u>work / work</u> 10 or 11 hours a day!
    (v.)   *(n.)*

Vocabulary in Context

Read the following sentences. Choose the correct word or phrase for each sentence. Fill in the blanks.

bored *(adj.)*	enjoys *(v.)*	quiet *(adj.)*

1. Please turn the TV off. I need a _____ place to study.

2. I usually watch a movie when I am _____.

3. Raina _____ her new apartment. It's very big and bright!

improves *(v.)*	performs *(v.)*	unhappy *(adj.)*

4. Susan is _____ in New York. She doesn't like big cities.

5. My sister is a great singer. She _____ her music all over the world.

6. Every day my English _____ because I always study hard.

decides *(v.)*	lessons *(n.)*	plays *(v.)*	throw away *(v.)*

7. My little brother _____ basketball very well.

8. We _____ the trash after we eat dinner.

9. The English _____ in this class are very interesting.

10. My mother plans the vacations for our family. She _____ where we will go.

Reading Skill

Understanding Time Order Words

Time order words show the sequence of events in a reading. Some time order words, for example, *first, second,* and *third,* are very clear. Other time order words, for example, *then, next, after that,* and *soon,* also show time order. It's important to understand these words and notice them when you read.

Put the sentences below in the correct order. Look back at the story to check your answers after you finish.

a. _____ After that, Nick begins to enjoy math.

b. _____ Then, they throw away the video games and move a thousand miles away.

c. _____ Soon, his schoolwork improves, and the other children's schoolwork does, too.

d. __1__ First, Shawn and Whitney decide to sell their house in Chicago.

e. _____ Next, Whitney decides to homeschool the children.

Topics for Discussion and Writing

1. Do you want to live in a large city or a small town? Explain your answer.

2. Can you play a musical instrument? Write about it. Or write about a musical instrument you want to play. Why do you want to play this instrument?

3. The Gray-Cabey family enjoys playing music together. What do you like to do with your family? Is it important to do this together? Why? Write a paragraph and give examples.

4. Write in your journal. Do you think the Gray-Cabey family has a better life now? Why or why not?

Critical Thinking

1. In this chapter, the parents make a decision and change their family's life. They move 1,000 miles away from a big city to a small town. This is a very big change. Work in a group. Imagine you are Shawn or Whitney. You are unhappy, but you *don't* want to move far away. What other ways can you change your lives? Discuss your ideas. Then complete the chart.

	Changes in . . .
our children's lives	
our lives	
our family's life	

2. The Gray-Cabey family moved to a different town. What changes did Shawn and Whitney make in their lives? Work with a partner and complete the chart.

Changes in Whitney's Life	Changes in Shawn's Life
1.	1.
2.	2.
3.	3.

3. Discuss these questions with a partner. What do you think is better for children, a large city or a small town? Why?

Cloze Quiz

Read the following passage. Fill in the blanks with the correct words from the list. Use each word only once.

begins	enjoy	improves	move	sell

First, Shawn and Whitney _____ (1) their house in Chicago. Then, they throw away the video games and _____ (2) 1,000 miles away to a very small town in Maine. Next, Whitney decides to "homeschool" the children. This means that she teaches them at home. After that, Nick _____ (3) to enjoy math. Soon, his schoolwork _____ (4), and the other children's schoolwork does, too. All the children _____ (5) their new lives, but sometimes they are bored.

decides	different	only	together	youngest

Shawn _____ (6) to give them music lessons. Now every afternoon, they play their music _____ (7). Each child plays a _____ (8) musical instrument. Nick is 16 years old. He plays the viola. Zack, who is 13 years old, plays the cello. Twelve-year-old Bryanna, the _____ (9) daughter in the family, plays the violin. The _____ (10) child in the family is Noah. He is only six years old, but he plays the piano very well.

Crossword Puzzle

Review the words in the box below. Then read the clues on the next page. Write the words in the correct spaces in the puzzle.

bored	happy	lessons	perform
decide	homeschool	move	together
different	improve	noisy	youngest
enjoy	instrument	oldest	

Crossword Puzzle Clues

ACROSS CLUES

5. The children sometimes _____ with their father. They are a five-person band.

6. The children _____ playing music. They think it's fun!

7. The children take music _____ from their father.

8. When we become better at something, we _____.

10. The children perform _____. They are a band.

12. The opposite of quiet

14. Noah is the _____ child in the family. All the other children are older than Noah.

15. A violin is a musical _____.

DOWN CLUES

1. The Gray-Cabey family is very _____ now. They like their new town very much.

2. Each child plays something _____. Nick plays the viola, Zack plays the cello, Bryanna plays the violin, and Noah plays the piano.

3. Shawn Cabey and Whitney Gray _____ their children. They do not send their children to school to learn.

4. We feel _____ when we do not have something interesting to do.

9. When I make a choice, I _____.

11. Nick is the _____ child. All the other children are younger than Nick.

13. Many families _____ from big cities to small towns.

Prereading

1. Look at the photograph. Work with a partner and answer the questions in the chart.

How many children are in the photo?	Are they brothers and sisters?
Number _____	Yes _____ No _____

2. Read the title of this story. This family is unusual. Why?
   a. They have young children.
   b. They have many young children.
   c. They have seven children the same age.

Reading

Read each paragraph carefully. Then answer the questions.

The McCaugheys: An Unusual Family

Septuplets!

Kenny and Bobbi McCaughey live in Iowa, in the United States. They have a very big family. In fact, they have eight children. But this family is also very unusual. They have septuplets! Septuplets are seven children who are born together. Their names are Brandon, Joel, Kelsey, Kenny, Natalie, Alexis, and Nathan. In this photo, they are all one year old. The McCaugheys also have another daughter. Her name is Mikayla. She is the oldest child in the family. In this photo, she is two and a half years old.

1. Who are Kenny and Bobbi McCaughey?
   a. The parents
   b. The children

2. They have a big family. **In fact**, they have eight children. **In fact** means
   a. however.
   b. in addition.
   c. really.

3. **Unusual** means
   a. large.
   b. special.
   c. young.

4. How many children do the McCaugheys have?
   a. Eight
   b. Seven
   c. Five

5. What are **septuplets**?
   a. Large families
   b. Seven children born together
   c. Five-year-old children

6. The McCaugheys also have **another** daughter. Her name is Mikayla.
   Another means
   a. older.
   b. younger.
   c. one more.

7. _____ True _____ False   Mikayla is a septuplet.

8. How old are the septuplets? _____

In the Beginning

It is hard work to take care of seven babies at the same time. Kenny and Bobbi do not take care of the seven babies alone. Many people help the family. In the beginning, babies do not sleep a lot. Every day, eight or nine people come to the McCaughey house to help them. Their friends and families help to feed, clean, and dress the babies. Every week, the septuplets use about 170 diapers! They drink a lot of milk, too.

9. Hard means
   a. fun.
   b. difficult.
   c. interesting.

10. Alone means
   a. carefully.
   b. with help.
   c. by yourself.

11. _____ True _____ False   Many people help Kenny and Bobbi.

12. _____ True _____ False   Babies sleep a lot in the beginning.

13. Friends and families help because septuplets
   a. are hard work.
   b. drink a lot of milk.
   c. are unusual.

14. Their friends and families help to feed, clean, and **dress** the babies.
   Dress means
   a. to put a dress on the babies.
   b. to put clothes on the babies.

15. Babies use **diapers** because they can't
   a. drink from a cup.
   b. use the bathroom.

16. What do you think the next paragraph will discuss?
   a. Other things that babies cannot do
   b. How Mikayla feels about having seven brothers and sisters
   c. The septuplets as they grow up

Five Years Later

Now the children are older. Bobbi says, "It's easy to take care of the children now. They feed and dress themselves, and they don't need diapers anymore!" This year, the septuplets are ready to start school. But the house will not be quiet. Why not? The children do not leave the house to go to school. Bobbi and Kenny homeschool the children. They go to school at home. Mikayla studies at home, too. "Homeschooling" is popular in the United States. Many families decide to teach their children at home. The McCaughey children do all their schoolwork at home. They have a classroom in their house, too.

17. It's easier to take care of the septuplets now because
   a. they are older.
   b. they go to school.
   c. their big sister helps.

18. _____ True _____ False   The septuplets wear diapers now.

19. The septuplets are unusual students because they
   a. are not ready to go to school.
   b. can't dress themselves.
   c. go to school at home.

20. Homeschooling is **popular**.
   Popular means
   a. many people like homeschooling.
   b. homeschooling is expensive.
   c. homeschooling is easy.

21. Who is the septuplets' teacher? _____

22. **Homeschooling** means that
   a. children do not learn.
   b. children do not have teachers.
   c. children learn at home.

23. Many families **decide** to teach their children at home. **Decide** means
   a. make a choice.
   b. think about.
   c. learn how.

The Septuplets Today

Now the septuplets are 17 years old. They go to high school, and they know how to drive. Soon they will be ready for college. Then the McCaughey house will finally be quiet!

24. They **know how to** drive. **Know how to** means
a. want to.
b. cannot.
c. can.

25. Then the McCaughey house will **finally** be quiet. **Finally** means
a. quickly.
b. after a long time.
c. never.

 Read the complete passage. Then answer the questions that follow.

CD 1
TR 5

The McCaugheys: An Unusual Family

Septuplets!

1   Kenny and Bobbi McCaughey live in Iowa, in the United States. They have a very
2   big family. In fact, they have eight children. But this family is also very unusual. They
3   have septuplets! Septuplets are seven children who are born together. Their names
4   are Brandon, Joel, Kelsey, Kenny, Natalie, Alexis, and Nathan. In this photo, they are
5   all one year old. The McCaugheys also have another daughter. Her name is Mikayla.
6   She is the oldest child in the family. In this photo, she is two and a half years old.

In the Beginning

7   It is hard work to take care of seven babies at the same time. Kenny and Bobbi do
8   not take care of the seven babies alone. Many people help the family. In the beginning,
9   babies do not sleep a lot. Every day, eight or nine people come to the McCaughey
10 house to help them. Their friends and families help feed, clean, and dress the babies.
11 Every week, the septuplets use about 170 diapers! They drink a lot of milk, too.

Five Years Later

12 Now the children are older. Bobbi says, "It's easy to take care of the children now.
13 They feed and dress themselves, and they don't need diapers anymore!" This year,

14 the septuplets are ready to start school. But the house will not be quiet. Why not? The
15 children do not leave the house to go to school. Bobbi and Kenny homeschool the
16 children. They go to school at home. Mikayla studies at home, too. "Homeschooling"
17 is popular in the United States. Many families decide to teach their children at home.
18 The McCaughey children do all their schoolwork at home. They have a classroom in
19 their house, too.

The Septuplets Today

20 Now the septuplets are 17 years old. They go to high school, and they know how
21 to drive. Soon they will be ready for college. Then the McCaughey house will finally
22 be quiet!

The teenaged septuplets in the family's driveway

Scanning for Information

Read the questions. Then go back to the complete passage and scan quickly for the answers. Circle the letter of the correct answer or write your answer in the space provided.

1. Where does the McCaughey family live?

_____

2. Who helps Kenny and Bobbi McCaughey take care of the young septuplets?

_____

3. What is very popular in the United States?

_____

4. Where do the children go to school now?

_____

5. What is the main idea of this passage?
   a. It is hard work for parents to take care of septuplets.
   b. Homeschooling is very popular today in the United States.
   c. The McCaugheys are unusual because they have septuplets.

Vocabulary Skill

Recognizing Word Forms

In English, some words can be either a noun (*n.*) or a verb (*v.*), for example, *change*.

Read the sentences below. Decide if the correct word is a noun or a verb. Circle your answer. Do the examples below as a class before you begin.

EXAMPLES:

a. Bobbi <u>changes / changes</u> a lot of diapers.
        (v.)   *(n.)*

b. They do many diaper <u>changes / changes</u> every day.
                (v.)   *(n.)*

1. Bobbi and Kenny do not get a lot of <u>sleep / sleep</u> in the beginning.
                                    (v.) *(n.)*

2. The septuplets do not <u>sleep / sleep</u> a lot at first.
                                       (v.)   (n.)

3. The family <u>uses / uses</u> a room in their house as a classroom.
                   (v.)   (n.)

4. That room has many <u>uses / uses</u>. It is a classroom, a playroom, and a living room.
                               (v.)   (n.)

5. Bobbi and Kenny <u>work / work</u> hard during the day.
                          (v.)   (n.)

6. They do a lot of <u>work / work</u> at night, too.
                       (v.)   (n.)

7. The septuplets have a good <u>start / start</u> in school because their parents teach them.
                              (v.)   (n.)

8. They usually <u>start / start</u> their schoolwork in the morning.
                 (v.)   (n.)

9. Their families <u>help / help</u> them with the children.
                  (v.)   (n.)

10. Now Bobbi and Kenny don't need a lot of <u>help / help</u> because the children are older.
                              (v.)   (n.)

Vocabulary in Context

Read the following sentences. Choose the correct word for each sentence. Fill in the blanks.

hard *(adj.)*	help *(v.)*	septuplets *(n.)*	together *(adv.)*

1. _____ are seven children who are born at the same time.

2. I meet my classmates on the bus, and we go to school _____.

3. My brother is a nurse. It is a very _____ job.

4. My teachers _____ me to learn English.

feeds *(v.)*	ready *(adj.)*	unusual *(adv.)*

5. Jim always _____ his dog before he goes to work.

6. It often rains in the spring, but snow is _____.

7. We always cook dinner early, and we are _____ to eat at 6:00 p.m.

| decide *(v.)* | popular *(adj.)* | teacher *(n.)* |

8. Class begins when the _____ comes into the room.

9. Ice cream is a _____ dessert in many countries.

10. Some students _____ to use laptops in class. Other students use notebooks.

Reading Skill

Understanding a Bar Graph

Bar graphs compare amounts or numbers. The bar graph below compares the number of multiple births in the United States in one year. Learning how to read bar graphs will help you understand important information about the topics in a reading.

Look at the bar graph below and answer the questions.

1. Look at the bar graph. Then circle the correct answers to complete the sentences below.
   a. Multiple births are more than <u>one baby / two babies</u> born together.
   b. There are more <u>quadruplet / twin</u> births than all other multiple births.
   c. Triplets are <u>three / four</u> babies born together.
   d. Quadruplets are <u>three / four</u> babies born together.
   e. <u>Quadruplets / Quintuplets and higher</u> are the smallest number of multiple births.

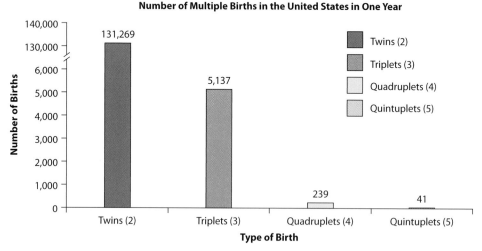

Number of Multiple Births in the United States in One Year

Source: National Organization of Mothers of Twins Clubs, Inc. (Multiple Births Statistics)

2. The bar graph shows the number of multiple births in the United States. Match each kind of multiple birth with the correct number.

41	239	5,137	131,269

a. _____ Twins
b. _____ Triplets
c. _____ Quadruplets
d. _____ Quintuplets and higher

Topics for Discussion and Writing

1. Bobbi and Kenny homeschool their children. What subjects do they teach? Work in pairs and write a schedule for the McCaughey school day.

_____

_____

_____

_____

_____

2. Do you think it is fun to be a septuplet? Why or why not? Discuss your ideas with your classmates.

3. Write in your journal. What do you think about homeschooling? Is it a good idea? Why or why not? Write a paragraph to explain your opinion.

A mother helps her son with his homework.

Critical Thinking

1. Work in a small group. The McCaughey's septuplets are seventeen years old now. How much food do you think they eat in one day? Decide on the amounts of food and drinks they need for each meal. Complete the chart.

	Breakfast	Lunch	Dinner
Drinks	1 gallon of orange juice		
Food			
Dessert			
Snacks			

2. Work in a group. Write a list of questions you want to ask the septuplets. Then exchange your list with another group. Try to answer the other group's questions.

Questions	Answers
1.	1.
2.	2.
3.	3.
4.	4.
5.	5.

3. Discuss these questions with a partner. Why do you think some people decide to homeschool their children? Discuss possible reasons. Do you think "homeschooling" is good for children? Why or why not?

Cloze Quiz

Read the following passage. Fill in the blanks with the correct words from the list. Use each word only once.

alone	feed	hard	help	milk

It is _____ (1) work to take care of seven babies at the same time. But Kenny and Bobbi do not take care of the seven babies _____ (2). Many people help the family. In the beginning, babies do not sleep a lot, so every day, eight or nine people come to the McCaughey house to _____ (3) them. Their friends and families help to _____ (4), clean, and dress the babies. Every week, the septuplets use about 170 diapers! They drink a lot of _____ (5), too.

decide	easy	leave	older	popular

Now the children are _____ (6). Bobbi says, "It's _____ (7) to take care of the children now. They feed and dress themselves, and they don't need diapers anymore." This year, the septuplets are ready to start school. But the house will not be quiet. Why not? The children do not _____ (8) the house to go to school. They go to school at home. Bobbi and Kenny homeschool the children. "Homeschooling" is _____ (9) in the United States. Many families _____ (10) to teach their children at home. The McCaughey children do all their schoolwork at home. They have a classroom in their house, too.

Crossword Puzzle

Review the words in the box below. Then read the clues on the next page. Write the words in the correct spaces in the puzzle.

another	feed	homeschooling	septuplets
decide	finally	Iowa	teacher
diapers	hard	older	together
dress	help	popular	unusual

Crossword Puzzle Clues

ACROSS CLUES

2. Bobbi is her children's _____. The children study at home with her.

4. Family and friends help to _____ the children breakfast, lunch, and dinner.

6. Homeschooling is very _____ in the United States. Many parents think it is a good idea.

8. The McCaughey family lives in _____. It is a state in the United States.

9. _____ are seven children who are born at the same time.

12. _____ is not unusual in the United States. Many parents teach their children at home.

15. The McCaugheys get _____ from their families and friends.

16. When the children were babies, they used 170 _____ every week.

DOWN CLUES

1. Did Kenny and Bobbi _____ to teach the children at home? Yes!

3. The McCaugheys have eight children. They do not want to have _____ child. They have enough!

5. The children can _____ themselves now. They can put on their clothes by themselves.

7. The McCaugheys are a very _____ family.

10. Septuplets are seven children born _____. They are born on the same day.

11. When all the children are at college, the house will _____ be very quiet!

13. Mikayla is _____ than the other seven children.

14. Feeding, dressing, and caring for eight children is _____ work.

UNIT 3

Learning and Memory

A young girl looks for a way out of a hedge maze.

1. What are some ways that people can learn? Are these helpful to you? Why or why not?

2. Can you improve your memory? How can you do this?

CHAPTER **5** It's OK to make mistakes!

Prereading

1. Read the title of this chapter. What will you read about?

a. Why people make mistakes

b. Why mistakes are important

c. Why mistakes can be helpful

2. Look at the photo.

The students in the photo

a. help each other.

b. work together.

c. learn new things.

d. All of the above

3. Complete this sentence:

I <u>like / don't like</u> to work with my classmates because _____.

Reading

Read each paragraph carefully. Then answer the questions.

It's OK to make mistakes!

Most teachers try to help their students as much as possible. Students ask questions when they don't understand the lesson. This is the best way to learn, right? Maybe not, says Dr. Manu Kapur. He is the director of the Learning Sciences Lab at the National Institute of Education of Singapore. "Don't be too quick to get help when you are learning something new. Try to work on it yourself first."

1. Most teachers try to help their students **as much as possible**.
   As much as possible means
   a. teachers help students a lot.
   b. teachers help students a little.
   c. teachers help students sometimes.

2. Why do students ask questions?
   a. They don't like the lesson.
   b. They don't understand the lesson.
   c. They understand the lesson.

3. _____ True _____ False   Dr. Kapur is a teacher.

4. "Don't be too **quick** to get help when you are learning something new."
   a. This sentence means
      1. ask for help first.
      2. don't ask for help first.
      3. don't make a mistake.
   b. **Quick** means
      1. fast.
      2. hard.
      3. happy.

5. "**Try to work on it yourself first**." This sentence means
   a. try to find the answer by yourself first.
   b. ask your teacher for help.
   c. ask your classmates for the answer.

Dr. Kapur believes that students learn best when they struggle. It's OK to make mistakes when you try to learn new information. Sometimes you will fail. Then, when you are successful, you will remember that information better. In other words, the failing helps you to succeed.

6. **Struggle** means to do something that is
   a. easy.
   b. difficult.
   c. new.

7. **Fail** means
   a. make a mistake.
   b. learn something new.
   c. do something correctly.

8. You will **remember** that information better. This means
   a. you will forget the information.
   b. you will not forget the information.
   c. you will understand the information.

9. When you **succeed,** you
   a. make mistakes.
   b. remember things correctly.
   c. accomplish something.

10. **Succeed** and **fail**
    a. are opposites.
    b. mean the same.

Dr. Kapur studies two groups of students in schools in Singapore. He gives difficult mathematical problems to the students in both groups. In the first group, the teacher helps the students to solve the problems. The students ask a lot of questions, and the teacher answers them. The teacher gives the students a lot of help. The students find the answers to the problems with the teacher's help. The second group of students receives the same mathematical problems, but the teacher doesn't help them. The students work with their classmates to solve the problems. The problems are difficult, but the students have many ideas. They talk together about the best way to solve the problems. Then both groups of students take a math test. The teachers correct the test, and they are surprised. Which group of students does better on the test?

11. A **group** means

    a. some students in a class.

    b. some teachers in a room.

    c. some mathematical problems.

12. _____ True _____ False   Dr. Kapur studies four groups of students.

13. **Difficult** means

    a. easy.

    b. hard.

    c. long.

14. What is an example of a **difficult mathematical problem**?

    a. $10 - 3 = x$

    b. $(1 + x)^n = 1 + \dfrac{nx}{1!} + \dfrac{n(n-1)x^2}{2!} + \cdots$

    c. $a^2 + b^2 = x$

15. The teacher helps the students in

    a. the first group.

    b. the second group.

    c. both groups.

16. The students work together in

    a. the first group.

    b. the second group.

    c. both groups.

17. The students work with their classmates to **solve** the problems. **Solve** means

    a. ask a question.

    b. help a classmate.

    c. find the answer.

18. The teachers correct the test, and they are **surprised**.

    a. The teachers are surprised because of

        1. the results.

        2. the students.

        3. the mathematical problems.

    b. **Surprised** means

        1. happy.

        2. unhappy.

        3. amazed.

19. What do you think the next paragraph will discuss?

    a. The group of students that does better

    b. The group of student that doesn't do better

Dr. Kapur says that the second group of students learns better. The students make mistakes, but they learn from their mistakes. "When we spend time on a problem, we begin to understand it better. This can help us in the real world."

20. The second group learns better because

    a. the students learn from their mistakes.

    b. the students are very smart.

    c. the teacher helps them.

21. When we **spend time** on a problem, we begin to understand it better. **Spend time** means

    a. do something quickly.

    b. do something slowly.

    c. do something correctly.

22. What is the **real world**?

    a. School and classroom life

    b. Family and work life

    c. Vacations and holidays

 Read the complete passage. Then answer the questions that follow.

CD 1
TR 6

It's OK to make mistakes!

1   Most teachers try to help their students as much as possible. Students ask questions
2 when they don't understand the lesson. This is the best way to learn, right? Maybe
3 not, says Dr. Manu Kapur. He is the director of the Learning Sciences Lab at the
4 National Institute of Education of Singapore. "Don't be too quick to get help when
5 you are learning something new. Try to work on it yourself first."
6   Dr. Kapur believes that students learn best when they struggle. It's OK to make
7 mistakes when you try to learn new information. Sometimes you will fail. Then, when
8 you are successful, you will remember that information better. In other words, the
9 failing helps you to succeed.

10 Dr. Kapur studies two groups of students in schools in Singapore. He gives difficult
11 mathematical problems to the students in both groups. In the first group, the teacher
12 helps the students to solve the problems. The students ask a lot of questions, and the
13 teacher answers them. The teacher gives the students a lot of help. The students find
14 the answers to the problems with the teacher's help. The second group of students
15 receives the same mathematical problems, but the teacher doesn't help them. The
16 students work with their classmates to solve the problems. The problems are difficult,
17 but the students have many ideas. They talk together about the best way to solve the
18 problems. Then both groups of students take a math test. The teachers correct the test,
19 and they are surprised. Which group of students does better on the test?

20 Dr. Kapur says that the second group of students learns better. The students make
21 mistakes, but they learn from their mistakes. "When we spend time on a problem, we
22 begin to understand it better. This can help us in the real world."

Students work together to solve a problem.

Scanning for Information

Read the questions. Then go back to the complete passage and scan quickly for the answers. Circle the letter of the correct answer.

1. Sometimes students do not understand a lesson. They usually
   a. do not say anything.
   b. ask their classmates.
   c. ask the teacher.

2. Does Dr. Kapur think this is the best way to learn something new?
   a. Yes
   b. No

3. Students remember new information when they
   a. ask the teacher questions.
   b. study harder.
   c. struggle and make mistakes.

4. Dr. Kapur studies two groups of students because
   a. he wants two groups to do the same thing.
   b. he wants the groups to do different things.
   c. one group together is too big.

5. Why are the teachers surprised that the second group does better?
   a. Because they think the second group doesn't study
   b. Because they think both groups will do well
   c. Because they think the first group will do better

6. What is the main idea of the story?
   a. Dr. Kapur believes that people learn better when they take time to work on a problem.
   b. Dr. Kapur believes that teachers are not very helpful to students.
   c. Dr. Kapur believes that students know more than teachers.

Vocabulary Skill

Recognizing Word Forms

In English, some words can be either a noun (n.) or a verb (v.), for example, *work*.

Read the sentences below. Decide if the correct word is a noun or a verb. Circle your answer. Do the examples as a class before you begin.

EXAMPLES:

a. Students need to <u>work / work</u> with their classmates first to solve problems.
      (v.)   (n.)

b. The <u>work / work</u> they do together helps them learn better!
   (v.)   (n.)

1. Student usually ask questions when they <u>struggle / struggle</u> with a difficult problem.
                                              (v.)   (n.)

2. When students work together, the <u>struggle / struggle</u> to solve a difficult problem becomes much easier!
                                      (v.)   (n.)

3. One student does not know the <u>answer / answer</u> to a math problem.
                              (v.)   (n.)

4. When the student asks questions, the other students in the group <u>answer / answer</u> them.
                                                      (v.)   (n.)

5. Dr. Kapur's <u>study / study</u> has some surprising information about learning.
         (v.)   (n.)

6. Dr. Kapur wants to <u>study / study</u> more students in the future.
                (v.) (n.)

7. Some students <u>mistake / mistake</u> the words *too* and *two*.
                  (v.)   (n.)

8. <u>Mistakes / Mistakes</u> are an important part of learning.
   (v.)   (n.)

Vocabulary in Context

Read the following sentences. Choose the correct word or phrase for each sentence. Fill in the blanks.

difficult *(adj.)*	fail *(v.)*	struggle *(v.)*

1. Students sometimes _____ tests when they don't understand the lesson.

2. My boss helps me when I _____ with my work.

3. It is _____ to walk to school in the snow.

quick *(adj.)*	remember *(v.)*	succeed *(v.)*

4. We can't find our classroom. Do you _____ the room number?

5. I study hard so I can _____ in college.

6. The walk to school is very _____. I get there in only ten minutes.

learn *(v.)*	mistakes *(n.)*	solve *(v.)*	surprised *(adj.)*

7. We _____ new words every day in class.

8. The students are _____. The college is closed because of the snow.

9. Michael and his wife _____ their problems together.

10. Marco sometimes makes _____ in class, but the teacher always corrects him.

Reading Skill

Creating a Flowchart

Flowcharts show the order of events or steps in a process. Creating a flowchart can help you understand and remember important information from a reading passage.

Refer back to the reading passage. Then read the list of actions for Dr. Kapur's study and the results below. Write them in the correct place in the flowchart.

- The students in the second group learn better.
- The teacher does not help the students to solve the problems.
- Both groups of students take a math test.
- When students spend time on a problem, they begin to understand it better.
- The teacher helps the students to solve the problems.

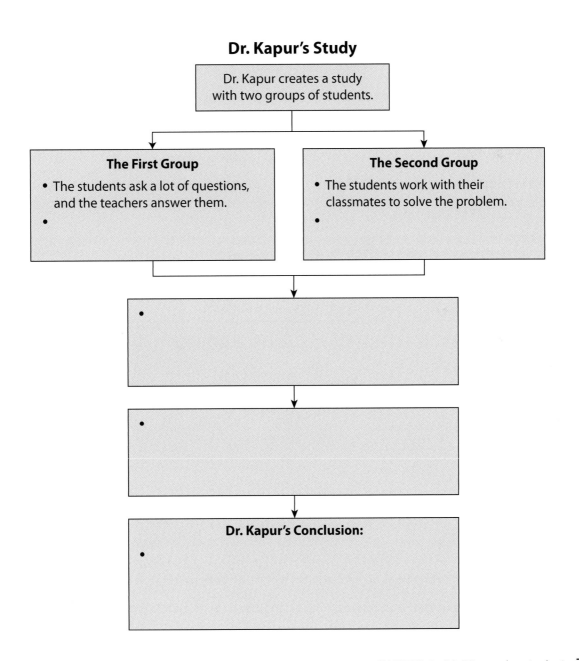

Dr. Kapur's Study

Dr. Kapur creates a study with two groups of students.

The First Group
- The students ask a lot of questions, and the teachers answer them.
-

The Second Group
- The students work with their classmates to solve the problem.
-

-

-

Dr. Kapur's Conclusion:
-

Topics for Discussion and Writing

1. Do you learn better when you ask the teacher to help you, or when you work with your classmates? Why do you think you learn better this way?

2. Dr. Kapur says, "When we spend time on a problem, we begin to understand it better." Do you agree with Dr. Kapur? Why or why not?

3. How does spending time on problems in class help us in the real world?

4. Write in your journal. Many students enjoy doing their homework together. Do you enjoy doing your homework with your classmates, or do you prefer to do homework alone? Why?

Critical Thinking

1. Think of a problem you have. How can you solve this problem? Write a list of steps to help you solve your problem.

2. Different people help you solve different problems. Work with a partner. Think of some kinds of problems you have. Who helps you with each kind of problem? Write your ideas in the chart.

What kinds of problem do you have?	Who can help you?
learning English in class	teachers and classmates

3. Discuss this with a partner: Working in a group can help us learn better. Do you agree? Why or why not?

Cloze Quiz

Read the following passage. Fill in the blanks with the correct words from the list. Use each word or phrase only once.

first	lesson	possible	questions	quick

Most teachers try to help their students as much as _____(1).
Students ask _____(2) when they don't understand the
_____(3). This is the best way to learn, right? Maybe not, says Dr. Manu
Kapur. He is the director of the Learning Sciences Lab at the National Institute of
Education of Singapore. "Don't be too _____(4) to get help when you are
learning something new. Try to work on it yourself _____(5)."

in other words	information	mistakes	struggle	successful

Dr. Kapur believes that students learn best when they _____(6). It's OK
to make _____(7) when you try to learn new _____(8).
Sometimes you will fail. Then, when you are _____(9), you will remember
that information better. _____(10), the failing helps you to succeed.

Crossword Puzzle

Review the words in the box below. Then read the clues on the next page. Write the words in the correct spaces in the puzzle.

classmates	learn	remember	study
difficult	mistakes	solve	succeed
fail	quick	struggle	surprised
group			

Crossword Puzzle Clues

ACROSS CLUES

2. I'm _____ that Leo isn't in class today. He is never absent.

5. The other students in my class are my _____.

6. I always forget vocabulary. I do not _____ new words very well.

9. Dr. Kapur did a _____ to find out how making mistakes can help students learn.

10. When I try to do something, but I cannot, I _____.

12. The opposite of slow

13. It's OK to _____ with new information. That is how we learn.

DOWN CLUES

1. If you keep trying, you will _____! Don't give up!

3. Can you help me _____ this math problem? I am having trouble with it.

4. Maria wants to _____ how to ride a bicycle.

7. If you do not make any _____ on the test, your score will be 100 percent.

8. Hard

11. The teacher wants us to work together in a _____ of four students.

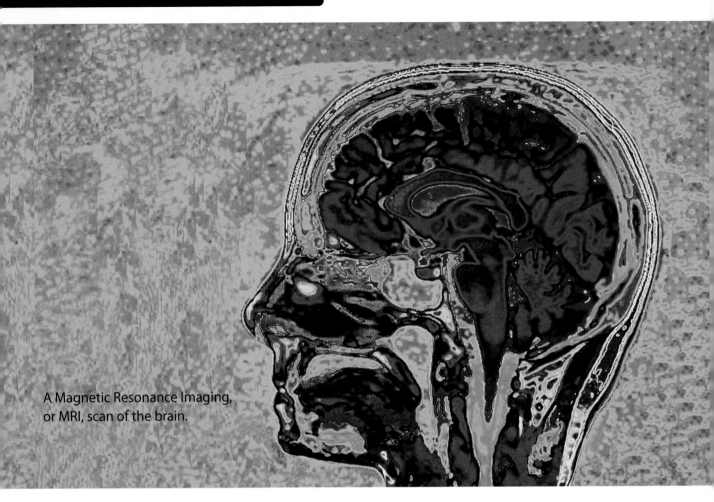

A Magnetic Resonance Imaging, or MRI, scan of the brain.

Prereading

1. Read the title of this chapter. What will you read about?

    a. A computer with a large memory

    b. A student with a good memory

    c. A person with a very unusual memory

2. What do you think a person with a super memory can remember?

    a. Important days and dates in his or her life

    b. Every day of his or her life

    c. Information from his or her classes and homework

3. Do you have a good memory or a bad memory? Why do you think this? Discuss your ideas with your classmates.

Reading

Read each paragraph carefully. Then answer the questions.

Super Memory

What is your earliest memory? Maybe it is your first day of nursery school. Maybe it is a special birthday. Most people usually have memories of different times in their childhood. But a few people, like Marilu Henner, can remember a lot more.

Marilu Henner is a famous American actress. However, Marilu Henner is famous for another reason, too. She has a super memory. She can remember everything that occurs in her life, even the weather. Doctors call this Highly Superior Autobiographical Memory (HSAM). People with HSAM can remember almost every day of their lives!

1. Your **childhood** is the period of life from
   a. birth to about one year.
   b. birth to about three years.
   c. birth to about 12 years.

2. Marilu Henner is famous because
   a. she is an actress.
   b. she has a super memory.
   c. Both a and b

3. She can remember everything that **occurs** in her life.
   a. She can remember
      1. important days in her life.
      2. her childhood.
      3. every day of her life.
   b. **Occurs** means
      1. happens.
      2. visits.
      3. sees.

4. Doctors call this Highly **Superior Autobiographical** Memory (HSAM).
   a. **Superior** means
      1. very clear.
      2. the same as others.
      3. higher than others.
   b. **Autobiographical** refers to
      1. your whole life.
      2. someone else's life.
      3. your childhood.

Dr. James McGaugh is a professor of neurobiology at the University of California. He is an expert on the brain and memory. Dr. McGaugh is the first doctor to discover and study superior autobiographical memory. Today he is quizzing Claire Jones to learn more about this subject. Dr. McGaugh asks Claire about the weather on a few dates ten years ago. "Let's see. It is slightly rainy and cloudy on January 15th and 16th. It is very hot on the weekend of the 26th and 27th, but no rain," says Claire. She also recalls the 15th as a Tuesday. Dr. McGaugh checks a calendar. Incredibly, Claire is right. She even remembers her dinner on that night ten years ago: "Chicken soup."

5. Dr. James McGaugh is an **expert** on the brain and memory. An **expert** is
   a. someone who studies a subject.
   b. someone who knows a lot about a subject.
   c. someone who is interested in a subject.

6. Today he is **quizzing** Claire Jones to learn more about **this subject**.
   a. **Quizzing** means
      1. asking questions.
      2. giving an exam.
      3. answering questions.
   b. **This subject** is
      1. the brain.
      2. neurobiology.
      3. superior autobiographical memory.

7. Dr. McGaugh **checks** a calendar.
   a. **Check** means
      1. make sure something is correct.
      2. put a (√) next to something.
      3. look at something.
   b. Why does Dr. McGaugh check a calendar?
      1. He wants to make sure that Claire is right.
      2. He wants to make an appointment.
      3. He thinks Claire is incorrect.

8. **Incredibly**, Claire is right. **Incredibly** means that something is
   a. very nice to know.
   b. difficult to believe, but true.
   c. very important information.

9. What do you think the next paragraph will discuss?
   a. More information about the things that Claire remembers
   b. More information about Dr. McGaugh's work
   c. More information about people with superior autobiographical memory

Obviously, not many people in the world have this kind of memory. "These people remember things that you and I can't possibly remember," McGaugh says. "They can recall something from many years ago as clearly as something you and I can recall about yesterday," McGaugh said, "but they can do it every day." People with HSAM remember 200 events or more in a year, while most people remember only about 8 to 11.

Why do some people have HSAM? Doctors are not sure, so they are studying the brains of people with super memory. This kind of memory lets you remember every day of your life. Unfortunately, it does not help you remember facts or figures. Scientists hope to learn how people can have super memories for other types of information. Perhaps scientists can help people become human computers one day!

10. **Obviously, not many people** in the world have this kind of memory.
    a. **Obviously** means
       1. of course.
       2. also.
       3. however.
    b. **Not many people** means
       1. several people.
       2. very few people.
       3. a couple of people.

11. "They can **recall** something from many years ago as clearly as something you and I can **recall** about yesterday."
    a. **Recall** means
       1. remember.
       2. tell.
       3. think about.
    b. People with HSAM remember things in the past
       1. but they don't remember yesterday.
       2. better than they remember yesterday.
       3. the same way that they remember yesterday.

12. People with HSAM remember 200 **events** or more in a year, **while** most people remember only about 8 to 11.

    a. An **event** is
       1. an important happening.
       2. a special birthday.
       3. a memory.

    b. **While** means
       1. and.
       2. but.
       3. so.

13. This kind of memory lets you remember every day of your life. **Unfortunately**, it does not help you remember **facts** or **figures**.

    a. **Unfortunately** means
       1. surprisingly.
       2. sadly.
       3. happily.

    b. **Facts** are
       1. details.
       2. people.
       3. truths.

    c. **Figures** are
       1. pictures.
       2. guesses.
       3. numbers.

 Read the complete passage. Then answer the questions that follow.

CD 1
TR 7

Super Memory

1   What is your earliest memory? Maybe it is your first day of nursery school. Maybe
2 it is a special birthday. Most people usually have memories of different times in their
3 childhood. But a few people, like Marilu Henner, can remember a lot more.

4   Marilu Henner is a famous American actress. However, Marilu Henner is famous
5 for another reason, too. She has a super memory. She can remember everything
6 that ever occurs in her life, even the weather. Doctors call this Highly Superior
7 Autobiographical Memory (HSAM). People with HSAM can remember almost every
8 day of their lives!

9 Dr. James McGaugh is a professor of neurobiology at the University of California.
10 He is an expert on the brain and memory. Dr. McGaugh is the first doctor to
11 discover and study superior autobiographical memory. Today he is quizzing Claire
12 Jones to learn more about this subject. Dr. McGaugh asks Claire about the weather
13 on a few dates ten years ago. "Let's see. It is slightly rainy and cloudy on January
14 15th and 16th. It is very hot on the weekend of the 26th and 27th, but no rain,"
15 says Claire. She also recalls the 15th as a Tuesday. Dr. McGaugh checks a calendar.
16 Incredibly, Claire is right. She even remembers her dinner on that night ten years
17 ago: "Chicken soup."

18 Obviously, not many people in the world have this kind of memory. "These people
19 remember things that you and I can't possibly remember," McGaugh says. "They can
20 recall something from many years ago as clearly as something you and I can recall
21 about yesterday," McGaugh said, "but they can do it every day." People with HSAM
22 remember 200 events or more in a year, while most people remember only about 8 to 11.

23 Why do some people have HSAM? Doctors are not sure, so they are studying
24 the brains of people with super memory. This kind of memory lets you remember
25 every day of your life. Unfortunately, it does not help you remember facts or
26 figures. Scientists hope to learn how people can have super memories for other
27 types of information. Perhaps scientists can help people become human
28 computers one day!

A collection of old photographs.

Scanning for Information

Read the questions. Then go back to the complete passage and scan quickly for the answers. Circle the letter of the correct answer or write your answer in the space provided.

1. How many events can most people remember in one year? _____

2. Why is Marilu Henner so famous? _____

3. What is HSAM? _____

4. What is Dr. James McGaugh an expert on? _____

5. Why is Dr. McGaugh asking Claire Jones questions? _____

6. How many events can people with HSAM remember? _____

7. What do scientists hope to learn about? _____

8. What is the main idea of this story?
    a. Super memory is not helpful for facts and figures.
    b. Marilu Henner is famous because she is an actress and she has super memory.
    c. Some people have super memory and can remember every day of their lives.

Vocabulary Skill

Recognizing Word Forms

In English, many adjectives *(adj.)* can become adverbs *(adv.)* by adding the suffix *-ly,* for example, *quick (adj.)* becomes *quickly (adv.).*

Read the sentences below. Decide if the correct word is an adjective or an adverb. Circle your answer. Do the examples as a class before you begin.

EXAMPLES:

a. Claire <u>quick / quickly</u> answers all of the doctor's questions.
        (adj.)   *(adv.)*

b. Claire's <u>quick / quickly</u> answers were all correct.
        (adj.)   *(adv.)*

1. Claire says, "It's raining slight / slightly right now."
   (adj.)   (adv.)

2. When Claire remembers the weather on January 15, she remembers a cloudy day with slight / slightly rain.
   (adj.)   (adv.)

3. Most people cannot possible / possibly remember every day of their lives.
   (adj.)   (adv.)

4. It's not possible / possibly for most people to recall more than 11 events in a year.
   (adj.)   (adv.)

5. Marilu Henner has an incredible / incredibly memory.
   (adj.)   (adv.)

6. Incredible / Incredibly, people with HSAM remember about 200 events in a year.
   (adj.)   (adv.)

7. Claire can clear / clearly describe the weather from days ten years ago!
   (adj.)   (adv.)

8. Her clear / clearly memories surprise Dr. McGaugh.
   (adj.)   (adv.)

9. Unfortunate / Unfortunately, HSAM doesn't help you to remember all kinds of information.
   (adj.)   (adv.)

10. It is unfortunate / unfortunately that only a few people have super memories.
    (adj.)   (adv.)

Vocabulary in Context

Read the following sentences. Choose the correct word or phrase for each sentence. Fill in the blanks.

expert *(n.)*	fact *(n.)*	recall *(v.)*

1. I lost my keys. I can't _____ where I put them.

2. It is a _____ that lightning always comes before thunder.

3. Our teacher is an _____ on English grammar. She knows everything about it.

event (n.)	incredibly (adv.)	occur (v.)

4. Carol's college graduation was an important _____ in her life.

5. Earthquakes _____ in countries all over the world.

6. This is a very big university. _____, there are more than 20,000 students here.

check (v.)	figures (n.)	subject (n.)	superior (adj.)

7. Psychology is an interesting _____. I want to study it in college.

8. Some students have a _____ ability to solve mathematical problems.

9. I usually use my calculator to see if the _____ are correct on my receipts.

10. I'm not sure what time class begins on Monday. I need to _____ my schedule.

Reading Skill

Understanding Adverbs

Certain adverbs connect ideas between sentences and express the writer's opinion. For example, *obviously* means something is clear and easy to understand. It also shows that the writer is certain about the information. *Incredibly* means that something is hard to believe or surprising. *Unfortunately* means that something is sad or unlucky. Read the examples:

Claire remembers that January 15th ten years ago is a Tuesday. Dr. McGaugh checks a calendar. **Incredibly**, *Claire is right.*

Claire even remembers dinner on January 15th ten years ago. **Obviously**, *not many people in the world have that kind of memory.*

HSAM lets you remember every day of your life. **Unfortunately**, *it does not help you remember facts or figures.*

Understanding these adverbs and noticing them when you read will help you understand important ideas in a reading.

Read the sentences below. Complete each sentence with *Obviously, Incredibly,* or *Unfortunately*.

1. John did not study all semester. _____, he passed the final exam.

2. I want to come to the party with you. _____, I have to work on Saturday, so I cannot come.

3. Susan is crying. _____, something is making her unhappy.

4. The little girl was lost in the woods for three days. _____, when her parents found her, she was all right.

5. Hanna needs to mail an important letter. _____, the post office is closed today.

6. Anna is checking her watch and looking down the street. _____, she is waiting for someone.

Topics for Discussion and Writing

1. What do you think are the advantages and disadvantages of a highly superior autobiographical memory?

2. Are there some memories that people may want to forget? Why do you think so?

3. What are some of the most important events in your life? Why are they important to you?

4. Write in your journal. What kinds of things do you want to remember? Why?

Graduates of all ages celebrate their achievement.

Critical Thinking

1. How can you improve your memory? Make a list. Then compare it with your classmates' lists.

2. Ask your classmates the question below. Write their names and answers in the chart.

Name of Classmate	What is your earliest memory?

3. Discuss these questions with a partner. Do you want to have a highly superior autobiographical memory? Why or why not?

Cloze Quiz

Read the following passage. Fill in the blanks with the correct words from the list. Use each word only once.

checks	expert	incredibly	occurs	superior

Marilu Henner is a famous American actress. However, Marilu Henner is famous

for another reason, too. She has a super memory. She can remember everything that

ever _____ in her life, even the weather. Doctors call this Highly
        (1)

Superior Autobiographical Memory (HSAM).

Dr. James McGaugh is a professor of neurobiology at the University of California. He is an _____ (2) on the brain and memory. Dr. McGaugh is the first doctor to discover and study _____ (3) autobiographical memory. Today he is quizzing Claire Jones to learn more about this subject. Dr. McGaugh asks Claire about the weather on a few dates ten years ago. "Let's see. It is slightly rainy and cloudy on January 15th and 16th. It is very hot on the weekend of the 26th and 27th, but no rain," says Claire. She also recalls the 15th as a Tuesday. Dr. McGaugh _____ (4) a calendar. _____ (5), Claire is right. She even remembers her dinner on that day ten years ago: "Chicken soup."

| events | figures | recall | unfortunately | while |

Obviously, not many people in the world have this kind of memory. "These people remember things that you and I can't possibly remember," McGaugh says. "They can _____ (6) something from many years ago as clearly as something you and I can recall about yesterday," McGaugh said, "but they can do it every day." People with HSAM remember 200 _____ (7) or more in a year, _____ (8) most people remember only about 8 to 11.

Why do some people have HSAM? Doctors are not sure, so they are studying the brains of people with super memory. This kind of memory lets you remember every day of your life. _____ (9), it does not help you remember facts or _____ (10). Scientists hope to learn how people can have super memories for other types of information. Perhaps scientists can help people become human computers one day!

Crossword Puzzle

Review the words in the box below. Then read the clues on the next page. Write the words in the correct spaces in the puzzle.

autobiographical	expert	incredibly	superior
check	facts	occur	unfortunately
childhood	figures	recall	while
event			

Crossword Puzzle Clues

ACROSS CLUES

1. People with _____ intelligence are not always happy. They wish they could be more normal.

4. I finished my math homework. Please _____ my answers to make sure they're correct.

6. John has four exams tomorrow, _____ I only have two exams.

9. When car accidents _____, it is important to call the police.

12. I want to have an _____ memory. I want to remember everything that happens in my life.

13. My 21st birthday was a very special _____ in my life.

DOWN CLUES

2. _____, I cannot go to the movie with you. I have to study for an exam.

3. Do you _____ your first day of school? I don't remember mine.

5. Your _____ is the time before you become a teenager.

7. The boy fell out of a window. _____, he was not badly hurt.

8. I do not understand these _____. How do these numbers add up?

10. If you have a question about nutrition, ask Anna. She is an _____ on healthy diets.

11. Some people have a good memory for _____, such as the names of historical people and important dates.

Big Cities and Small Towns

People walk through a colorful street in Hong Kong after a rainstorm.

1. Is your hometown a big city or a small town? Is it a good place to live? Why or why not?

2. Do you want to live in a big city or a small town? Which is better for you? Why?

Prereading

1. Look at the photograph. What are the people doing?
   a. They are cleaning a new house.
   b. They are moving into a new house.
   c. They are leaving a new house.

2. Why is this family doing this? Write one reason here. Discuss some reasons with your classmates.

   _____

   _____

3. Work with a partner. Read the title of this chapter. Where is the best place to live? Why do you think so? Complete the chart.

	The Best Place to Live	Reasons
You		
Your Partner		

Reading

Read each paragraph carefully. Then answer the questions.

The Best Place to Live

Do you like your hometown? Are you happy there? Most Americans like their hometowns. In fact, 80 percent of Americans say that they like their hometowns very much. They are happy there. A large number of Americans—almost 40 percent—live in the same place all their lives. They never move to a different place. However, some other Americans are ready for a change.

1. _____ True _____ False   Most Americans are happy in their hometowns.

2. **In fact** means
    a. fortunately.
    b. really.
    c. mostly.

3. _____ True _____ False   Most Americans live in the same place all their lives.

4. **Some other Americans are ready for a change** means
    a. they want a new job.
    b. they want a new place to live.
    c. they want to change their clothes.

Forty-six percent of all Americans say they want to live in a different location. They like their hometowns, but they want to move to a new place. For example, some people live in a city, but they want to live in a small town. Some city dwellers want to move to a rural area, or countryside. They don't like cities. Other people want to live in the suburbs. Suburbs are places near cities. However, many people who live in small towns and rural areas are not happy either. They prefer to live in a different kind of place.

5. **Forty-six percent of all Americans** means
   a. many Americans.
   b. all Americans.
   c. a few Americans.

6. A **location** is
   a. a town.
   b. a city.
   c. a place.

7. **City dwellers** are people who
   a. live in a city.
   b. work in a city.
   c. live at home.

8. Other people want to live in the **suburbs**, which are areas near cities.
   The **suburbs** are
   a. in cities.
   b. close to cities.
   c. far from cities.

9. **However, many people who live in small towns and rural areas are not happy either.**
   Who isn't happy?
   a. Some people who live in small towns
   b. Some people who live in rural areas
   c. Both a and b

10. A **rural area** is in
   a. a city.
   b. the countryside.
   c. a town.

11. They **prefer** to live in a different kind of place.

    Prefer means

    a. like something more.
    b. like something a lot.
    c. like something the same.

12. What do you think the next paragraph will discuss?

    a. Everyone agrees on the best place to live.
    b. Some people do not agree on the best place to live.

Of course, not everyone agrees on the best place to live. Different people choose to live in different places. For instance, young people prefer to live in cities. They choose big cities like New York, Boston, and Los Angeles. Martin Beck agrees with this. He lives in Boston. "I love to live in the city," says Martin. "There are great museums, restaurants, and movie theaters. There are a lot of jobs here, too."

13. **Of course** means

    a. differently.
    b. happily.
    c. naturally.

14. _____ True _____ False   All Americans agree on the best place to live.

15. _____ True _____ False   Martin Beck is a young person.

16. Where does Martin live?

    a. In a small town
    b. In a big city
    c. In a museum

17. Does Martin like where he lives?

    a. Yes
    b. No
    c. I don't know.

On the other hand, many older Americans prefer to live in smaller towns. For example, Janet and Mario Miller and their family live in a small town in Idaho. Janet says, "I love our town! We know all of our neighbors. The schools here are small and the streets are always quiet." Yet the majority of Americans—young and old—agree on one idea: They prefer warm weather to cold weather.

Some people dream about moving to a different place, but most people are happy with their hometowns. Where do you want to live?

18. **On the other hand** shows
    a. a new idea.
    b. an opposite idea.
    c. something you are holding.

19. Who prefers to live in smaller towns?
    a. All older Americans
    b. All Americans
    c. Some older Americans

20. _____ True _____ False   Janet and Mario Miller are older Americans.

21. Where does the Miller family live?
    a. In a big city
    b. In a warm place
    c. In a small town

22. Janet says, "I love our town! We know all of our **neighbors**."
    Neighbors are people who
    a. work with you.
    b. live near you.
    c. go to school with you.

23. Yet the **majority** of Americans—young and old—agree on one idea: They prefer warm weather to cold weather.
    Majority means
    a. some.
    b. all.
    c. most.

24. Which sentence is correct?
    a. Most Americans like warm weather better than cold weather.
    b. Most Americans like cold weather better than warm weather.

25. **Some people dream about moving to a different place, but most people are happy with their hometowns.**
    This sentence means
    a. most people do not want to move to a different place.
    b. most people want to move to a different place.
    c. most people will be happy in a different place.

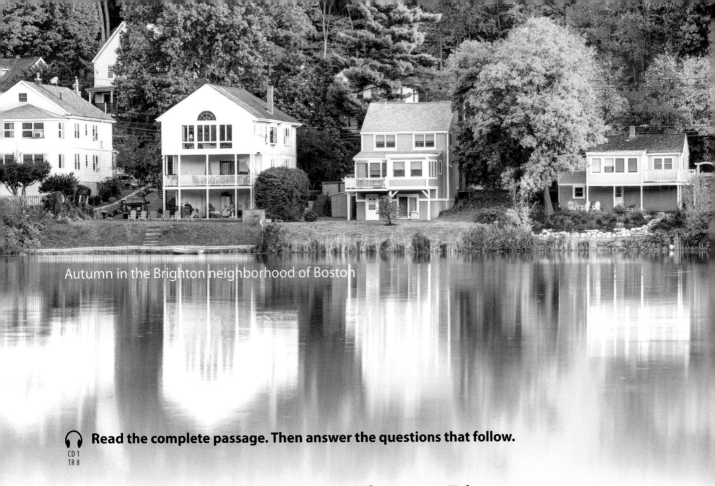
Autumn in the Brighton neighborhood of Boston

Read the complete passage. Then answer the questions that follow.

CD 1
TR 8

The Best Place to Live

1 Do you like your hometown? Are you happy there? Most Americans like their
2 hometowns. In fact, 80 percent of Americans say that they like their hometowns very
3 much. They are happy there. A large number of Americans—almost 40 percent—live
4 in the same place all their lives. They never move to a different place. However, some
5 other Americans are ready for a change.
6 Forty-six percent of all Americans say they want to live in a different location. They
7 like their hometowns, but they want to move to a new place. For example, some people
8 live in a city, but they want to live in a small town. Some city dwellers want to move
9 to a rural area, or countryside. They don't like cities. Other people want to live in the
10 suburbs. Suburbs are places near cities. However, many people who live in small towns
11 and rural areas are not happy either. They prefer to live in a different kind of place.
12 Of course, not everyone agrees on the best place to live. Different people choose to
13 live in different places. For instance, young people prefer to live in cities. They choose
14 big cities like New York, Boston, and Los Angeles. Martin Beck agrees with this. He
15 lives in Boston. "I love to live in the city," says Martin. "There are great museums,
16 restaurants, and movie theaters. There are a lot of jobs here, too."

17 On the other hand, many older Americans prefer to live in smaller towns. For
18 example, Janet and Mario Miller and their family live in a small town in Idaho. Janet
19 says, "I love our town! We know all of our neighbors. The schools here are small and
20 the streets are always quiet." Yet the majority of Americans—young and old—agree
21 on one idea: They prefer warm weather to cold weather.
22 Some people dream about moving to a different place, but most people are happy
23 with their hometowns. Where do you want to live?

Scanning for Information

Read the questions. Then go back to the complete passage and scan quickly for the answers. Circle the letter of the correct answer or write your answer in the space provided.

1. Complete each sentence with the correct number.
   a. _____ percent of Americans want to live in a different place.
   b. _____ percent of Americans never move to a different place.
   c. _____ percent of Americans like their hometowns a lot.

2. a. Where do some young people prefer to live?

   _____

   b. What are some reasons for this?
      1. _____
      2. _____
      3. _____
      4. _____

3. a. Where do some older people prefer to live?

   _____

   b. What are some reasons for this?
      1. _____
      2. _____
      3. _____

4. What is the main idea of this passage?
   a. A large number of Americans live in the same place all their lives.
   b. Many older Americans prefer to live in the city.
   c. Most Americans are happy where they live, but some are ready for a change.

Vocabulary Skill

Recognizing Word Forms

In English, some adjectives *(adj.)* become nouns *(n.)* by adding the suffix *-ness*, for example, kind *(adj.)*, kindness *(n.)*.

Read the sentences below. Decide if the correct word is an adjective or a noun. Circle your answer. Do the examples below as a class before you begin.

EXAMPLES:

a. Bob is a shy / shyness person. He is quiet and does not talk to his classmates very often.
   (adj.) (n.)

b. Bob doesn't have many friends because of his shy / shyness.
   (adj.) (n.)

1. Some people live in very small / smallness apartments in New York City.
   (adj.)   (n.)

2. Only 3,000 people live in my hometown. I know everyone there because of the small / smallness of the town.
   (adj.)   (n.)

3. Many families enjoy the quiet / quietness of life in a rural area.
   (adj.)   (n.)

4. There are very few cars, trucks, or people. The countryside is really a very quiet / quietness place to live.
   (adj.)   (n.)

5. Most Americans do not enjoy the cold / coldness of the winter.
   (adj.)   (n.)

6. They often stay indoors on very cold / coldness days. They prefer the summer!
   (adj.)   (n.)

7. Many Americans are ready / readiness to move to a new place.
   (adj.)   (n.)

8. Many Americans' ready / readiness to move to a new place is not unusual.
   (adj.)   (n.)

9. Many families with young children like to live in small towns and are very happy / happiness.
   (adj.)   (n.)

10. The children's happy / happiness is important.
    (adj.)   (n.)

Vocabulary in Context

Read the following sentences. Choose the correct word or phrase for each sentence. Fill in the blanks.

change *(n.)*	hometown *(n.)*	on the other hand	prefer *(v.)*

1. Steven loves his _____. He never wants to move to another city.

2. Leigh sometimes feels lonely because she lives away from her parents. _____, she loves her job and apartment in her new city.

3. Tara will go to a new school next year. It will be a big _____ for her.

4. I _____ the winter because I don't like hot weather.

agrees *(v.)*	dweller *(n.)*	location *(n.)*	majority *(n.)*	neighbors *(n.)*

5. Kim loves living in New York City. She will always be a city _____.

6. Marta thinks Italian food is delicious, and Jack _____ with her.

7. The _____ of Americans drinks coffee with their breakfast.

8. My _____ always help me when I have a problem in my home.

9. My home is in a great _____. There are many stores and restaurants here.

Reading Skill

Reading a Pie Chart
Pie charts contain important information about a topic. They show percentages or parts of a whole.

Look at the pie charts below and answer the questions.

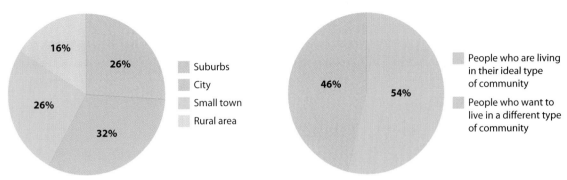

Source: www.pewsocialtrends.org

1. Where does the largest percentage of Americans live? _____

2. Where does the smallest percentage of Americans live? _____

3. What percentage of Americans live near a city?
   a. 26%
   b. 52%
   c. 57%

4. Are the majority of Americans happy where they live?
   a. Yes
   b. No

Topics for Discussion and Writing

1. Work with a partner. What are some reasons that people choose different places to live? Make a list with your partner. Discuss some of your reasons with your class.

2. What is most important to you when you choose a place to live? Why is this important? Explain your answer.

3. Do you think it is difficult or easy to move to a new place? Why? Write your answer and discuss it with your classmates.

4. Write in your journal. Do you like your city? Why or why not? Give reasons for your answer.

Critical Thinking

1. Ask your classmates the following questions and write their answers in the chart.

Survey of the Best Place to Live			
Name of student			
Where do you live?			
Are you happy there?			
Why or why not?			
Do you want to live in another place?			
Why or why not?			
Where do you want to live?			

2. Compare your chart with your classmates' charts. Then discuss these questions with your class.
   a. Are most of your classmates happy where they live? Why or why not?
   b. Where do most students want to live? Why?
   c. What is more important to happiness, where you live or who you live with? Why?
      Give reasons for your answers.

Cloze Quiz

Read the following passage. Fill in the blanks with the correct words from the list. Use each word only once.

change	happy	hometowns	move	place

Do you like your hometown? Are you _____ (1) there? Most Americans like their hometowns. In fact, 80 percent of Americans say that they like their _____ (2) very much. They are happy there. A large number of Americans—almost 40 percent—live in the same _____ (3) all their lives. They never _____ (4) to a different place. However, some other Americans are ready for a _____ (5).

countryside	dwellers	location	prefer	town

Forty-six percent of all Americans say they want to live in a different _____ (6). They like their hometowns, but they would like to move to a new place. For example, some people live in a city, but they want to live in a small _____ (7). Some city _____ (8) want to move to a rural area, or _____ (9). They don't like cities. However, many people who live in small towns and rural areas are not happy either. They _____ (10) to live in a different kind of place.

Crossword Puzzle

Review the words in the box below. Then read the clues on the next page. Write the words in the correct spaces in the puzzle.

agree	hand	naturally	prefer
change	hometown	neighbors	rural
dweller	location	percent	suburbs
fact	majority	place	

Crossword Puzzle Clues

ACROSS CLUES

1. The people next door are very nice _____.

5. A city with many museums is a wonderful _____ to live!

9. I _____ with you. I like big cities, too.

10. Shanghai, China, has a lot of people. In _____, it has the highest population of any city in the world.

14. _____ means of course.

15. About 54 _____ of Americans like where they live.

DOWN CLUES

2. Cities have many advantages. On the other _____, they are often very crowded.

3. The _____ are very close to the city. We like living there.

4. Where do you _____ to live? In a big city or a small town?

6. The park is a good _____ for a party. My backyard is too small.

7. The _____ of people I know like living in small towns.

8. Barbara is a city _____. She loves living in a big city.

11. John really likes his _____. He does not want to move.

12. Kate prefers to live in a _____ area. She likes the countryside.

13. I want to _____ where I live. I don't like living here.

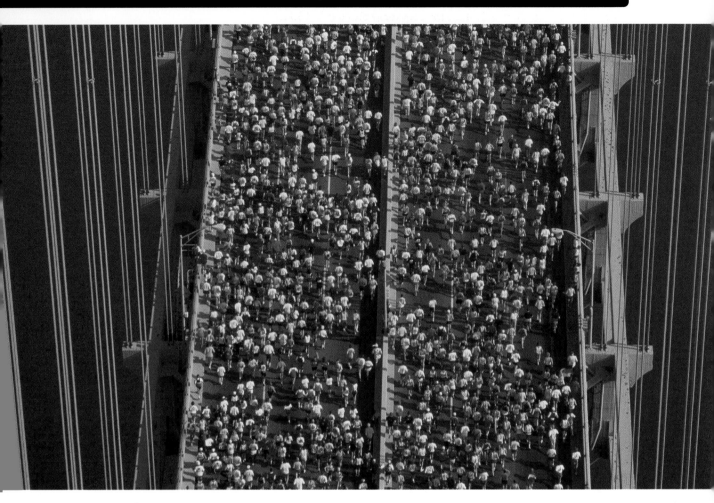

Prereading

1. Look at the photo. How many people do you think are running in this marathon?

2. Read the title of this chapter. Why is the New York City Marathon a world race? Where is this race? Who runs in this race?

3. Is a big city a good place for a marathon? Why or why not?

4. Work with two or three classmates. What are some reasons why people run in marathons? Make a list. Compare your list with your other classmates' lists.

[1]**marathon:** a foot race about 26 miles (about 42 kilometers) long

Reading

Read each paragraph carefully. Then answer the questions.

The New York City Marathon: A World Race

Fred Lebow started the New York City Marathon in 1970. It began as a small, unimportant race. Only 127 people ran, and just 55 of them finished. They ran around Central Park four times. Only a few people watched them run. However, over the years, the marathon grew and became more popular.

Today, people come from all over the world to run in the marathon. Runners must be at least 18 years old. That is a requirement. However, there is no age limit. In fact, the oldest runner was an 89-year-old man. Recently, more than 50,000 people ran in the New York City Marathon. Large crowds cheered the runners and offered them cold drinks. The crowds also encouraged the runners to run faster. This encouragement was very helpful to the runners.

1. Only 127 people ran, and **just** 55 of them finished.
   Just means
   a. because.
   b. only.
   c. more than.

2. _____ True _____ False   All 127 people finished the first marathon.

3. However, **over the years**, the marathon grew and became more popular.
   Over the years means
   a. as the years went by.
   b. one year after.
   c. many more years.

4. _____ True _____ False   Runners cannot be younger than 18 years old.

5. Runners must be at least 18 years old. That is a **requirement.**
   A **requirement** is something that is
   a. a choice.
   b. necessary.
   c. old.

6. **There is no age limit** means
   a. people of any age can run.
   b. older people cannot run.
   c. anyone older than 18 years old can run.

7. Large crowds **cheered** the runners. **Cheer** means
    a. watch carefully.
    b. shout happily.
    c. take photographs.

8. The crowds also **encouraged** the runners to run faster. **Encourage** means that the crowds
    a. give the runners cold drinks.
    b. give the runners support.
    c. make the runners feel happy.

9. What do you think the next paragraph will discuss?
    a. Other changes in the New York City Marathon
    b. Other people who run in the marathon
    c. Marathons in other cities

The course of the marathon changed, too. Instead of running around Central Park, the participants go through the five boroughs of New York City: Queens, Brooklyn, Manhattan, the Bronx, and Staten Island. The marathon begins at the beginning of the Verrazano-Narrows Bridge in Staten Island. The runners go across the bridge into Brooklyn. Then they go up through Queens and into the Bronx. The marathon finishes in Central Park in Manhattan. The complete course is 26.2 miles. The best runners finish in less than three hours.

10. The **course** of the marathon changed, too. In this sentence, **course** means
    a. route.
    b. class.
    c. reason.

11. **Instead of** running around Central Park, the participants go through the five boroughs of New York City. **Instead of** means
    a. in addition to.
    b. in place of.
    c. around.

12. _____ True _____ False   The fastest runners finish the race in three hours or more.

Although there are some changes to the New York City Marathon, it is always exciting. In the past, many unusual events happened during the marathon. For example, Pat Tuz and Jon Weilbaker got married a few minutes before the race. Then they ran the race with their wedding party. Some people run the whole marathon as a family. Other people run the race backwards. In the fall of 1992, Fred Lebow, the founder of the New York City Marathon, slowly ran his last race. He was very ill with cancer, but he did not want to stop running. In October 1994, Fred died. However, the New York City Marathon, and all its excitement, will continue for many years to come.

13. **Although** there are some changes to the New York City Marathon, it is always exciting. **Although** means
   a. and.
   b. because.
   c. but.

14. In the past, many unusual **events** happened during the marathon. An **event** is
   a. a race.
   b. a wedding.
   c. a happening.

15. **Other people run the race backwards**. This means that some people
   a. move along on their backs.
   b. run facing the opposite direction.
   c. run very slowly.

16. _____ True _____ False   Pat Tuz and Jon Weilbaker ran the marathon backwards.

17. _____ True _____ False   Fred Lebow ran his last race in 1994.

18. **In the fall** of 1992, Fred Lebow, the founder of the New York City Marathon, slowly ran his last race.
   In the fall means
   a. when someone fell down.
   b. the time before winter.
   c. the beginning of the year.

The fastest runners in the New York City Marathon lead the way through Brooklyn.

CD 1
TR 9

Read the complete passage. Then answer the questions that follow.

The New York City Marathon: A World Race

1   Fred Lebow started the New York City Marathon in 1970. It began as a small,
2 unimportant race. Only 127 people ran, and just 55 of them finished. They ran around
3 Central Park four times. Only a few people watched them run. However, over the
4 years, the marathon grew and became more popular.

5   Today, people come from all over the world to run in the marathon. Runners must
6 be at least 18 years old. That is a requirement. However, there is no age limit. In
7 fact, the oldest runner was an 89-year-old man. Recently, more than 50,000 people
8 ran in the New York City Marathon. Large crowds cheered the runners and offered
9 them cold drinks. The crowds also encouraged the runners to run faster. This
10 encouragement was very helpful to the runners.

11   The course of the marathon changed, too. Instead of running around Central Park,
12 the participants go through the five boroughs of New York City: Queens, Brooklyn,
13 Manhattan, the Bronx, and Staten Island. The marathon begins at the beginning of

14　the Verrazano-Narrows Bridge in Staten Island. The runners go across the bridge into
15　Brooklyn. Then they go up through Queens and into the Bronx. The marathon finishes
16　in Central Park in Manhattan. The complete course is 26.2 miles. The best runners
17　finish in less than three hours.
18　　Although there are some changes to the New York City Marathon, it is always
19　exciting. In the past, many unusual events happened during the marathon. For
20　example, Pat Tuz and Jon Weilbaker got married a few minutes before the race. Then
21　they ran the race with their wedding party. Some people run the whole marathon as
22　a family. Other people run the race backwards. In the fall of 1992, Fred Lebow, the
23　founder of the New York City Marathon, slowly ran his last race. He was very ill with
24　cancer, but he did not want to stop running. In October 1994, Fred died. However,
25　the New York City Marathon, and all its excitement, will continue for many
26　years to come.

Scanning for Information

Read the questions. Then go back to the complete passage and scan quickly for the answers. Circle the letter of the correct answer or write your answer in the space provided.

1. Describe two ways that the New York City Marathon changed.

a. _____

b. _____

2. What do the crowds do during the marathon?

a. _____

b. _____

3. What are some unusual events that happened during the marathon?

a. _____

b. _____

4. What is the main idea of this story?

a. The New York City Marathon began in 1970.

b. The founder of the New York City Marathon was an important man.

c. The New York City Marathon is a very popular and exciting race.

Vocabulary Skill

Recognizing Word Forms

In English, some verbs *(v.)* can become nouns *(n.)* by adding the suffix *-ment*, for example, *agree (v.)*, *agreement (n.)*.

Read the sentences below. Decide if the correct word is a noun or a verb. Circle your answer. Do the examples as a class before you begin.

EXAMPLES:

a. Everyone <u>agrees / agreement</u> that the marathon is exciting.
         (v.)   *(n.)*

b. My friend and I have an <u>agree / agreement</u> to run in the marathon next year.
                (v.)   *(n.)*

1. The crowds <u>excite / excitement</u> the runners in the marathon.
          (v.)   *(n.)*

2. There is a lot of <u>excite / excitement</u> all day.
              (v.)   *(n.)*

3. Many people <u>encourage / encouragement</u> the runners by cheering.
           (v.)   *(n.)*

4. The crowd's <u>encourage / encouragement</u> is very important to the runners.
            (v.)   *(n.)*

5. You must be 18 years old to run in the New York City Marathon. This is a <u>require / requirement</u>.
                                           (v.)   *(n.)*

6. The New York City Marathon <u>requires / requirement</u> a lot of planning.
                   (v.)   *(n.)*

7. Some marathon runners <u>improve / improvement</u> their speed every year.
               (v.)   *(n.)*

8. This <u>improves / improvement</u> is exciting to many runners.
         (v.)   *(n.)*

Vocabulary in Context

Read the following sentences. Choose the correct word or phrase for each sentence. Fill in the blanks.

cheer (v.)	encouragement (n.)	instead of

1. The crowds _____ a lot during baseball games.

2. I want to go swimming, but it is raining. _____ going to the beach, I will go to the indoor swimming pool at the college.

3. My parents always believed I could succeed. Their _____ helped me to do well in school.

course (n.)	just (adv.)	limit (n.)	popular (adj.)

4. Marathons are very _____ in American cities.

5. The speed _____ on this highway is 55 miles an hour. You cannot drive faster than 55.

6. Olivia runs two miles every day. She follows a _____ through the park near her home.

7. I am taking _____ one class this semester because I have a job. I don't have time to take more than one class.

however	requirement (n.)	unusual (adj.)

8. Snow is _____ in New York City in April. It very rarely happens.

9. Robert is only 17. He has to wait one year to meet the age _____ for the New York City Marathon.

10. It is usually very cold in January. _____, this year it was mild.

Reading Skill

Understanding a Line Graph

It's important to learn to read line graphs. They contain important information about a reading. The line graphs below help you understand information about the story.

The following line graph shows the number of participants in the New York City Marathon from 1970 through 2014. Look at it carefully and then read the statements. Circle True or False.

New York City Marathon—Number of Runners

Source: www.tcsnycmarathon.org/about-the-race/results/finisher-demographics

1. More than 15,000 people ran in the New York City Marathon in 1980.
   a. True
   b. False

2. About 24,000 people ran in the New York City Marathon in 1990.
   a. True
   b. False

3. Almost 30,000 people ran in the New York City Marathon in 2000.
   a. True
   b. False

4. More than 45,000 people ran in the New York City Marathon in 2010.
   a. True
   b. False

5. The largest increase in the number of runners occurred from 1970 to 1980.
   a. True
   b. False

6. The smallest increase in the number of runners occurred from 1990 to 2000.
   a. True
   b. False

The following line graph shows the winning finishing times of the men and women participants in the New York City Marathon from 1970 through 2014. Look at it carefully. Then read the sentences that follow. Complete each sentence with the word *women* or *men* to make it correct.

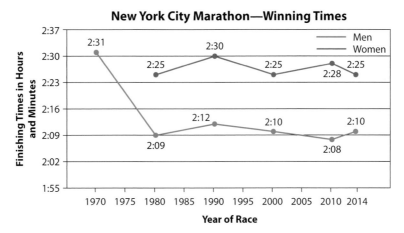

New York City Marathon—Winning Times

Source: www.tcsnycmarathon.org/results

7. In 1970, only _____ finished the marathon.

8. In 1980, the winning time for _____ was 2 hours, 9 minutes.

9. In 1990, the winning time for _____ was 2 hours, 30 minutes.

10. In 2010, the winning time for _____ was 2 hours, 28 minutes.

11. In 2014, the winning time for _____ was 2 hours, 10 minutes.

Topics for Discussion and Writing

1. Work with two or three classmates. Did you or your partners ever run in a marathon? If so, how did you prepare for it? What was the race like? If not, do you want to? Why or why not?

2. Imagine that your friend wants to run in a marathon. In your group, discuss some advice that you can give your friend. Compare your suggestions with your other classmates' suggestions. Which suggestions are the best? Write a letter to your friend and give him or her your advice.

3. Write in your journal. Describe a popular sports event in your country. What is the event? Who participates? Why do people enjoy watching it?

Critical Thinking

1. What is your favorite activity? In a group, discuss what you each like to do the most, for example, play soccer, run, play tennis, cycle, swim. Make a list and compare it with your classmates' lists.

2. Discuss this question with a partner: People come from all over the world to run in the New York City Marathon. Why do you think they do this?

Cloze Quiz

Read the following passage. Fill in the blanks with the correct words from the list. Use each word only once.

cheered	limit	oldest	runners
encouragement	marathon	recently	

Today, people come from all over the world to run in the _____.
                                                                    (1)

Runners must be at least 18 years old. That is a requirement. However, there is no age

_____. In fact, the _____ runner was an 89-year-old
        (2)   (3)

man. _____, more than 50,000 people ran in the New York City
        (4)

Marathon. Large crowds _____ the runners and offered them cold
                              (5)

drinks. The crowds also encouraged the _____ to run faster. This
                                              (6)

_____ was very helpful to the runners.
        (7)

| backwards | events | exciting | ran |
| changes | example | race | whole |

Although there are some _____ (8) in the New York City Marathon,

it is always _____ (9). In the past, many unusual _____ (10)

happened during the marathon. For _____ (11), Pat Tuz and Jon

Weilbaker got married a few minutes before the _____ (12). Then they

_____ (13) the race with their wedding party. Some people run the

_____ (14) marathon as a family. Other people run the race

_____ (15).

Crossword Puzzle

Review the words in the box below. Then read the clues on the next page. Write the words in the correct spaces in the puzzle.

although	encouragement	limit	runner
backwards	event	oldest	unusual
cheer	instead	race	winning
course	just	requirement	

Crossword Puzzle Clues

ACROSS CLUES

1. A marathon is a _____ that is 26.2 miles or 42.165 kilometers.

2. The fastest _____ time in the New York City Marathon was 2 hours 5 minutes 6 seconds.

7. The _____ runner in the New York City Marathon was an 89-year-old man.

9. Running in a marathon when you are 89 years old is very _____!

11. When I say you can do something, I am offering you _____.

12. The New York City Marathon is only one exciting _____ that takes place in New York during the year.

14. _____ I want to run in the New York City Marathon next year, I don't have time to get ready.

DOWN CLUES

1. You must be at least 18 years old to run in the New York City Marathon. That is a _____.

3. The marathon route goes through all the five boroughs _____ of only around Central Park.

4. The _____, or route, of the marathon changed. It no longer only goes around Central Park.

5. Most runners move forward in the race, but a few people run _____.

6. Every _____ in the race gets a number.

8. There is no age _____ for the New York City Marathon. You can run even if you are 100 years old!

10. The people watching the race _____ as the runners pass by.

13. I can't speak to you right now. I have _____ five minutes to catch the train. I don't want to be late.

Remarkable Researchers

Divers in Tulum, Mexico, retrieve the skull of "Naia," a teenage girl who died 12,000–13,000 years ago.

1. What kinds of science do you know about? Which kinds do you think are interesting? Why?

2. Who are some important scientists? Why are they important?

Dr. Margaret Mead greets the Samoans.

Prereading

1. Look at the photo. The woman on the right was Margaret Mead. She was American. Work with a partner to answer these questions.

   a. What kind of work did Margaret Mead do?
      1. She helped sick people.
      2. She painted pictures.
      3. She studied different groups of people.

   b. Where did Margaret Mead do most of her work?
      1. In her own country
      2. In different countries
      3. In different cities

2. Describe the kind of work that you think Margaret Mead did. Write one or two sentences.

   _____

   _____

3. Read the title of this chapter. Why do you think the whole world was Margaret Mead's home? How can the world be a person's home?

_____

_____

Reading

Read each paragraph carefully. Then answer the questions.

Margaret Mead: The World Was Her Home

Margaret Mead was a famous American anthropologist. She was born on December 16, 1901, in Philadelphia, Pennsylvania. She lived with her parents, her grandmother, and her brother and sisters. Her parents were both teachers. Her grandmother was a teacher, too. They believed that education was very important for children. They also believed that the world was important. Margaret learned many things from her parents and grandmother.

When she was a child, Margaret Mead's family traveled often and lived in many different towns. Margaret was always interested in people and places, so she decided to study anthropology in college to learn about different cultures. At that time, it was not very common for women to study in a university. It was even more unusual for women to study anthropology.

1. Margaret Mead was a **famous** American anthropologist. **Famous** means that
   a. many people knew about her.
   b. she was very experienced.
   c. she made a lot of money.

2. _____ True _____ False   Margaret Mead's parents were anthropologists.

3. A **culture** is a group of people who
   a. speak the same language.
   b. have the same customs and traditions.
   c. work together in the same place.

4. **Anthropologists** study different
   a. cultures.
   b. universities.
   c. kinds of travel.

5. **Common** means
   a. different.
   b. exciting.
   c. usual.

6. What do these two paragraphs discuss?
   a. Margaret's education as a young child
   b. The importance of Margaret's family and childhood
   c. The importance of Margaret's occupation

7. Why did Margaret decide to study anthropology?

   _____

8. What do you think the next paragraphs will discuss?
   a. Margaret Mead's interesting classes in college
   b. Margaret Mead's personal life after college
   c. Margaret Mead's work as an anthropologist after college

Mead graduated from college in 1923. She wanted to continue her education in anthropology, so she decided to go to American Samoa to study the young women there. Many people did not know about the culture of American Samoa. Mead wanted to learn about Samoans so that the world could learn about them, too.

Mead lived in Samoa for nine months and learned the language. She talked with the Samoan people, especially the teenage girls. She ate with them, danced with them, and learned many details about their peaceful culture.

9. _____ True _____ False   Mead went to Samoa to continue her education in anthropology.

10. Why did Mead want to learn about the Samoan culture?
    a. She wanted to go to college in Samoa.
    b. She wanted to teach the world about Samoa.
    c. She wanted to learn the Samoan language.

11. She ate with them, danced with them, and learned many **details** about their **peaceful** culture.
    a. **Details** means
       1. examples.
       2. specific information.
       3. kinds of dances.
    b. **Peaceful** means
       1. exciting.
       2. calm.
       3. interesting.

12. How long did Mead live in Samoa? _____

13. _____ True _____ False   Mead knew the Samoan language before she went to Samoa.

14. She talked with the Samoan people, **especially** the **teenage girls**.
   a. **Especially** means
      1. only.
      2. most importantly.
      3. except for.
   b. **Teenage girls** are
      1. 13 to 19 years old.
      2. 7 to 14 years old.
      3. over 18 years old.

15. _____ True _____ False   The Samoan culture was peaceful.

When Mead returned to the United States, she wrote a book about the young Samoan women she studied. The book was called *Coming of Age in Samoa,* and it was very popular. As a result, Margaret Mead became very famous. Before Mead wrote her book, people were not very interested in anthropology. Because of Mead's book, anthropology became a popular subject.

Margaret Mead studied many different cultures in her life. She continued to work, travel, write, and teach until she died in 1978. She was a remarkable woman of the world.

16. *Coming of Age in Samoa* was
   a. a book.
   b. a magazine.
   c. a movie.

17. What was the subject of Margaret's book?

_____

18. Why did Margaret Mead become famous?
   a. Because she was an anthropologist
   b. Because she studied many cultures
   c. Because she wrote a popular book

19. Margaret Mead continued to work, travel, write, and teach **until** she died in 1978.

   a. **Until** means
      1. when something begins.
      2. when something continues.
      3. when something ends.

   b. Complete the sentence: Last night Elizabeth studied at the library **until**
      1. it opened.
      2. it closed.
      3. she woke up.

20. Margaret Mead was a **remarkable** woman of the world.
   Remarkable means
      a. educated.
      b. hardworking.
      c. amazing.

Read the complete passage. Then answer the questions that follow.

CD 1
TR 10

Margaret Mead:
The World Was Her Home

1 Margaret Mead was a famous American anthropologist. She was born on December
2 16, 1901, in Philadelphia, Pennsylvania. She lived with her parents, her grandmother,
3 and her brother and sisters. Her parents were both teachers. Her grandmother was
4 a teacher, too. They believed that education was very important for children. They
5 also believed that the world was important. Margaret learned many things from her
6 parents and grandmother.
7   When she was a child, Margaret Mead's family traveled often and lived in many
8 different towns. Margaret was always interested in people and places, so she decided
9 to study anthropology in college to learn about different cultures. At that time, it was
10 not very common for women to study in a university. It was even more unusual for
11 women to study anthropology.
12   Mead graduated from college in 1923. She wanted to continue her education in
13 anthropology, so she decided to go to American Samoa to study the young women
14 there. Many people did not know about the culture of American Samoa. Mead wanted
15 to learn about Samoans so that the world could learn about them, too.

Mead lived in Samoa for nine months and learned the language. She talked with the Samoan people, especially the teenage girls. She ate with them, danced with them, and learned many details about their peaceful culture.

When Mead returned to the United States, she wrote a book about the young Samoan women she studied. The book was called *Coming of Age in Samoa,* and it was very popular. As a result, Margaret Mead became very famous. Before Mead wrote her book, people were not very interested in anthropology. Because of Mead's book, anthropology became a popular subject.

Margaret Mead studied many different cultures in her life. She continued to work, travel, write, and teach until she died in 1978. She was a remarkable woman of the world.

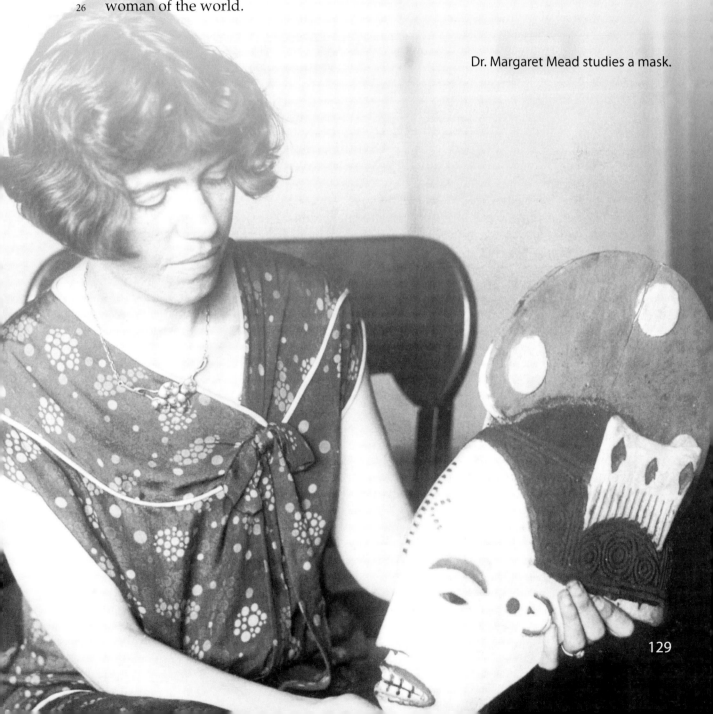

Dr. Margaret Mead studies a mask.

Scanning for Information

Read the questions. Then go back to the complete passage and scan quickly for the answers. Circle the letter of the correct answer or write your answer in the space provided.

1. Margaret Mead decided to study anthropology in college to learn about different cultures.

    a. Why do you think she made this decision?

    _____

    b. Was this an unusual decision? Why or why not?

    _____

2. How did Margaret study the Samoan people?

    _____

3. Why was Margaret Mead important to anthropology?

    _____

    _____

4. What is the main idea of this passage?

    a. Margaret Mead was interested in different cultures.

    b. Margaret Mead wrote a book about Samoan women.

    c. Margaret Mead helped to make anthropology a popular subject.

Margaret Mead with a model of a New Guinea village

Vocabulary Skill

Recognizing Word Forms

In English, some verbs *(v.)* become nouns *(n.)* by adding the suffix -*ence* or –*ance*, for example, *depend (v.), dependence (n.); appear (v.), appearance (n.)*.

Read the sentences below. Decide if the correct word is a verb or a noun. Circle your answer. Do the examples below as a class before you begin.

EXAMPLES:

a. When Margaret was a child, she depended / dependence on her parents for everything.
                              (v.)   *(n.)*

b. This depended / dependence continued until she completed high school.
         (v.)   *(n.)*

1. The Samoan women's appeared / appearance was different from Margaret's.
                    (v.)   *(n.)*

2. The Samoan people appeared / appearance to be friendly.
               (v.)   *(n.)*

3. Many people avoided / avoidance studying anthropology before Margaret Mead wrote
              (v.)   *(n.)*
her book.

4. Mead disliked their avoided / avoidance of anthropology.
             (v.)   *(n.)*

5. Life in Samoa differed / difference from life in the United States.
              (v.)   *(n.)*

6. Because of the differed / differences, many people wanted to read Margaret's book.
               (v.)   *(n.)*

Vocabulary in Context

Read the following sentences. Choose the correct word or phrase for each sentence. Fill in the blanks.

believe *(v.)*	especially *(adv.)*	remarkable *(adj.)*

1. Helen enjoys all her classes, but she _____ likes her English class. That is her favorite subject.

2. Sharks are _____ animals. They hunt for food at night by feeling movement in the water.

3. My brother and I exercise every day. We _____ that exercise is important for good health.

as a result	cultures *(n.)*	peaceful *(adj.)*

4. The Samoans are very _____ people. They rarely disagree or fight with each other.

5. Choi and Marina come from different _____, but they are very good friends.

6. Maria did not do her homework last night. _____, she was not prepared for class today.

details *(n.)*	interested *(adj.)*	popular *(adj.)*	until *(prep.)*

7. That is a very _____ type of car. Many people buy it because it is inexpensive and reliable.

8. Cesar is _____ in medicine. He wants to become a doctor.

9. I studied last night _____ midnight. Then I went to sleep.

10. There was an earthquake in California this morning, but I don't know the _____. I want to listen to the radio to learn more about it.

Reading Skill

Using a Timeline

Timelines show the time order of events, such as important dates in history or in a person's life. Using a timeline can help you understand and remember information from a reading passage. On a timeline, the earliest event is on the left. The most recent event is on the right.

Look at the dates on the timeline below. Go back to the reading on pages 128–129 and the illustration on this page. Write information about Margaret Mead's life on the timeline below next to the correct date.

The Life of Margaret Mead

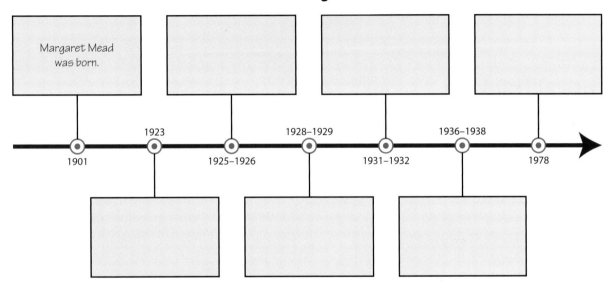

Margaret Mead was born.

1901   1923   1925–1926   1928–1929   1931–1932   1936–1938   1978

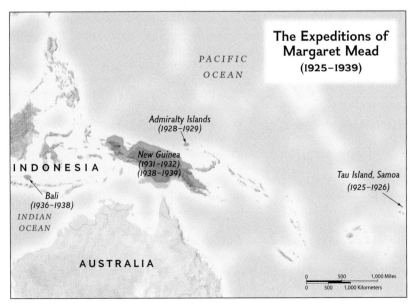

The Expeditions of Margaret Mead (1925–1939)

PACIFIC OCEAN

Admiralty Islands (1928–1929)

New Guinea (1931–1932) (1938–1939)

INDONESIA

Bali (1936–1938)

INDIAN OCEAN

Tau Island, Samoa (1925–1926)

AUSTRALIA

0   500   1,000 Miles
0   500   1,000 Kilometers

Topics for Discussion and Writing

1. Write a paragraph. Describe one or two interesting things you have learned about American culture. How did you learn these things about American culture?

2. Describe someone important in your culture. This may be someone who is alive now or who lived in the past. Write a paragraph about this person. When you are finished, exchange papers with a classmate and read each other's descriptions. Then discuss what you learned about your classmate's culture by reading about this person.

3. Do you think anthropology is an important science? Why or why not? Write a paragraph to explain your opinion. Give examples.

4. Write in your journal. Imagine that you are a student of anthropology. Decide what culture you want to study. Discuss your reasons in a paragraph.

Critical Thinking

1. Refer back to the *Prereading* section. Read your description of the work that you thought Margaret Mead did. How accurate was your description?

2. Work with two or three classmates. Imagine that you are a team of anthropologists. You are going to a new country to study a different culture. You plan to interview the people there to learn about their culture. What do you want to learn about this culture? What questions can you ask to get this information? Together, make a list of questions for your interview. When you are finished, write your questions on the board. Discuss all the groups' questions. As a class, make up one questionnaire.

3. Use your questionnaire to interview someone from a culture that is different from your own. You may interview someone in your class, but a person outside your class is better. Bring the answers back to class. Discuss what you learned from your interview.

4. Discuss these questions with a partner. Do you think it's important to learn about different cultures? Why or why not?

Cloze Quiz

Read the following passage. Fill in the blanks with the correct words from the list. Use each word only once.

about	decided	graduated	study
culture	education	learn	

Mead _____ (1) from college in 1923. She wanted to continue her

_____ (2) in anthropology, so she _____ (3) to go to

American Samoa to _____ (4) the young women there. Many people did

not know about the _____ (5) of American Samoa. Mead wanted to learn

_____ (6) Samoans so that the world could _____ (7) about

them, too.

because	interested	result	subject
book	popular	returned	wrote

When Mead _____ (8) to the United States, she

_____ (9) a book about the young Samoan women she studied.

The _____ (10) was called *Coming of Age in Samoa*, and it was very

_____ (11). As a _____ (12), Margaret Mead became very

famous. Before Mead wrote her book, people were not very _____ (13) in

anthropology. _____ (14) of Mead's book, anthropology became a popular

_____ (15).

Crossword Puzzle

Review the words in the box below. Then read the clues on the next page. Write the words in the correct spaces in the puzzle.

anthropologist	especially	peaceful	teenage
books	famous	popular	until
cultures	important	remarkable	world
details	interested	Samoa	

Crossword Puzzle Clues

ACROSS CLUES

3. The ages from 13 to 19 are the _____ years.

5. Margaret Mead was a very _____ author. Many people liked to read her books.

6. The library has many _____ by Margaret Mead.

9. Margaret Mead's books include many interesting _____ about the lives of other people. For example, they include information about their music, clothes, and food.

11. Margaret Mead was a very _____ woman. She was amazing.

13. I am very _____ in your last trip. Please tell me about it.

14. She is very busy. She can't meet with you _____ next month.

15. We enjoy studying about the _____ of different groups of people.

DOWN CLUES

1. An _____ is a person who studies different groups of people.

2. Margaret Mead's first book made her _____. Before that, not many people knew about her.

4. American _____ was the first place Margaret Mead went to after she graduated from college.

7. We like to travel, _____ to new and different places.

8. It is _____ to learn about other people's lives and traditions.

10. This is a _____ country. The people are gentle and kind.

12. Margaret Mead traveled all over the _____.

Prereading

1. Look at the picture. This man was Louis Pasteur.
   a. What kind of work did he do?
      1. He was an inventor.
      2. He was a scientist.
      3. He was a medical doctor.
   b. Where did Louis Pasteur do his work?
      1. In a laboratory
      2. In a hospital
      3. In an office

2. Read the title of this chapter.

    a. How is modern scientific work different from scientific work that people did hundreds of years ago?

    b. Why do you think Louis Pasteur was a modern-day scientist?

Reading

Read each paragraph carefully. Then answer the questions.

Louis Pasteur: A Modern-Day Scientist

In the summer of 1885, a sick dog attacked nine-year-old Joseph Meister. The dog had rabies, a deadly disease. Joseph became very ill after the attack. His doctor tried to help him, but there was no cure for rabies at that time. The doctor told Joseph's parents that perhaps there was one man who could save Joseph's life. His name was Louis Pasteur.

1. A **disease** is

    a. a summer activity.

    b. an attack by an animal.

    c. an illness or a sickness.

2. What is **rabies**?

    a. A deadly illness

    b. An animal attack

    c. A sick dog

3. a. Was Joseph's doctor able to help him?

      1. Yes

      2. No

    b. Why or why not?

4. A **cure** for a disease is
   a. a medicine or treatment that makes the disease go away.
   b. a careful description of that disease in a book.
   c. a special doctor who knows about that disease.

5. **His** name was Louis Pasteur. Who does **his** refer to?
   a. Joseph's parents
   b. Joseph's doctor
   c. The man who could save Joseph's life

6. What do you think the next paragraphs will discuss?
   a. Joseph's life after he became well again
   b. The life of Joseph's doctor
   c. Louis Pasteur's life

When Pasteur was a young boy in France, he was very curious. He was especially interested in medicine, so he spent many hours every day with the chemist who lived in his small town. The chemist sold pills, cough syrups, and other types of medicine, just as modern pharmacists, or druggists, do today. At that time, the chemist had to make all of the medicine himself. Young Louis enjoyed watching the chemist as he worked and listening to him assist the customers who came to him each day. Pasteur decided that one day he wanted to help people, too.

As a schoolboy, Pasteur worked slowly and carefully. At first, his teachers thought that young Louis might be a slow learner. Through elementary school, high school, and college, Pasteur worked the same thoughtful way. In fact, he was not a slow learner, but a very intelligent young man. He became a college professor and a scientist, and he continued to work very carefully.

7. Louis was **especially** interested in medicine, **so** he spent many hours every day with the chemist who lived in his small town.
   a. **Especially** means
      1. very.
      2. probably.
      3. originally.
   b. **So** means
      1. because.
      2. as a result.
      3. all the time.

8. Louis was very **curious**. He enjoyed watching the chemist as he worked and listening to the chemist **assist** his customers.

    a. **Curious** means
        1. hardworking.
        2. careful.
        3. interested in learning.
    b. **Assist** means
        1. help.
        2. sell.
        3. work.

9. Why did Louis spend many hours with the chemist?

    a. He was interested in medicine.
    b. He wanted to become a doctor.
    c. The chemist needed his help.

10. The chemist sold pills, cough syrups, and other types of medicine, **just as** modern **pharmacists,** or druggists, **do today**.

    a. **Just as** means
        1. only.
        2. the same as.
        3. whereas.
    b. **Pharmacists** are _____.
    c. What do pharmacists do today?

    _____

11. **As a schoolboy**, Pasteur worked slowly and carefully. **At first**, his teachers thought that young Louis might be a slow learner.

    a. **As a schoolboy** means
        1. Louis acted like a little boy.
        2. when Louis was a boy in school.
        3. boys in school work slowly.
    b. **At first** means
        1. in the beginning.
        2. one time.
        3. for one reason.
    c. Why did his teacher think Louis might be a slow learner?

    _____

12. _____ True _____ False   Louis was a slow learner and not an intelligent man.

13. _____ True _____ False   Louis continued to work very carefully when he became a professor and a scientist.

14. What do you think the next paragraph will discuss?
    a. Louis Pasteur's personal life
    b. Louis Pasteur's chemical discoveries
    c. Louis Pasteur's work as an adult

Because of Pasteur's patient methods, he was able to make many observations about germs. For example, germs cause meat and milk to spoil. They also cause many serious diseases. Pasteur was studying about the germs that cause rabies when Joseph Meister became ill. In fact, Pasteur believed he had a cure for rabies, but he had never treated a person with it before. At first, Pasteur was afraid to treat Joseph, but his doctor said the child was dying. Pasteur gave Joseph an inoculation, or shot, every day for ten days. Slowly, the child became better. Pasteur's vaccination cured him.

15. Germs cause meat and milk to **spoil**.
    Spoil means
    a. become warm.
    b. become rotten.
    c. become cold.

16. Pasteur gave Joseph an **inoculation**, or shot, **every day for ten days**.
    a. What is an **inoculation**?

    _____

    b. **Every day for ten days** means
       1. ten shots every day.
       2. one shot after ten days.
       3. one shot each day for ten days.

17. Why did the child become better?

    _____

During his lifetime, Pasteur studied germs and learned how they cause diseases in animals and people. He developed vaccinations that prevent many of these illnesses. He also devised the process of pasteurization, which stops food such as milk from spoiling. Louis Pasteur died on September 28, 1895, at the age of 72. Modern medicine continues to benefit from the work of this great scientist.

18. **During his lifetime** means
    a. in the years that he lived.
    b. after he became a college professor.
    c. when Joseph Meister was ill.

19. **Prevent** means
    a. describe something carefully.
    b. help something happen.
    c. stop something from happening.

20. What can **vaccinations** do?
    a. Help keep animals and people healthy
    b. Cause illnesses
    c. Stop food from spoiling

21. Pasteur **devised** the **process of pasteurization**.
    a. **Devised** means
       1. named.
       2. invented.
       3. liked.
    b. A **process** is a
       1. medical treatment.
       2. way to make money.
       3. specific way of doing something.
    c. The **process of pasteurization**
       1. prevents disease.
       2. causes illnesses.
       3. prevents milk from spoiling.

22. **Modern medicine** continues to **benefit** from the work of this great scientist.
    a. **Modern medicine** means
       1. medicine in the past.
       2. medicine today.
       3. vaccinations.
    b. When we **benefit** from something, we
       1. get an advantage.
       2. get a disadvantage.

Louis Pasteur laboratory equipment

🎧 **Read the complete passage. Then answer the questions that follow.**

CD 1
TR 11

Louis Pasteur:
A Modern-Day Scientist

1　　In the summer of 1885, a sick dog attacked nine-year-old Joseph Meister. The dog
2　had rabies, a deadly disease. Joseph became very ill after the attack. His doctor tried
3　to help him, but there was no cure for rabies at that time. The doctor told Joseph's
4　parents that perhaps there was one man who could save Joseph's life. His name was
5　Louis Pasteur.
6　　When Pasteur was a young boy in France, he was very curious. He was especially
7　interested in medicine, so he spent many hours every day with the chemist who lived
8　in his small town. The chemist sold pills, cough syrups, and other types of medicine,
9　just as modern pharmacists, or druggists, do today. At that time, the chemist had to
10　make all of the medicine himself. Young Louis enjoyed watching the chemist as he

11 worked and listening to him assist the customers who came to him each day. Pasteur
12 decided that one day he wanted to help people, too.

13   As a schoolboy, Pasteur worked slowly and carefully. At first, his teachers thought
14 that young Louis might be a slow learner. Through elementary school, high school,
15 and college, Pasteur worked the same thoughtful way. In fact, he was not a slow
16 learner, but a very intelligent young man. He became a college professor and a
17 scientist, and he continued to work very carefully.

18   Because of Pasteur's patient methods, he was able to make many observations
19 about germs. For example, germs cause meat and milk to spoil. They also cause many
20 serious diseases. Pasteur was studying about the germs that cause rabies when Joseph
21 Meister became ill. In fact, Pasteur believed he had a cure for rabies, but he had never
22 treated a person with it before. At first, Pasteur was afraid to treat Joseph, but his
23 doctor said the child was dying. Pasteur gave Joseph an inoculation, or shot, every
24 day for ten days. Slowly, the child became better. Pasteur's vaccination cured him.

25   During his lifetime, Pasteur studied germs and learned how they cause diseases in
26 animals and people. He developed vaccinations that prevent many of these illnesses.
27 He also devised the process of pasteurization, which stops food such as milk from
28 spoiling. Louis Pasteur died on September 28, 1895, at the age of 72. Modern medicine
29 continues to benefit from the work of this great scientist.

Scanning for Information

**Read the questions. Then go back to the complete passage and scan quickly for the answers.
Circle the letter of the correct answer or write your answer in the space provided.**

1. Why did Pasteur decide he wanted to help people?

    _____

    _____

2. What were some of Pasteur's observations about germs?
    a. _____
    b. _____

3. What was Joseph's illness?

    _____

4. Why did Pasteur agree to treat Joseph?

_____

_____

5. What is the main idea of this story?
   a. Louis Pasteur saved Joseph Meister's life by developing a cure for rabies.
   b. Louis Pasteur was a great scientist whose work continues to help science today.
   c. Louis Pasteur learned about germs and developed the process of pasteurization.

Vocabulary Skill

Recognizing Word Forms

In English, some verbs *(v.)* become nouns *(n.)* by dropping the final -*e* and adding the suffix *-ion*, for example, *graduate (v.), graduation (n.)*.

Read the sentences below. Decide if the correct word is a noun or a verb. Circle your answer. Do the examples below as a class before you begin.

EXAMPLES:

   a. Louis became a college professor after he graduated / graduation from the university.
                                                       (v.)   *(n.)*

   b. The Pasteur family was very happy at Louis's graduated / graduation.
                                                     (v.)   *(n.)*

1. Louis Pasteur's educates / education included watching the chemist.
              (v.)   *(n.)*

2. The chemist educated / education Louis to help people.
              (v.)   *(n.)*

3. Pasteur developed vaccinate / vaccinations for several serious diseases.
                  (v.)   *(n.)*

4. In most countries, doctors vaccinate / vaccinations children before they begin school.
                      (v.)   *(n.)*

5. Louis continued / continuation to work carefully in high school and college.
           (v.)   *(n.)*

6. The <u>continued / continuation</u> of his slow, careful work helped him learn a lot about germs.
        (v.)   *(n.)*

7. Pasteur <u>observed / observation</u> germs in people and animals.
            (v.)   *(n.)*

8. These <u>observe / observations</u> helped him develop vaccines.
         (v.)   *(n.)*

Vocabulary in Context

**Read the following sentences. Choose the correct word or phrase for each sentence.
Fill in the blanks.**

at first	because of	cure *(n.)*	decided *(v.)*

1. Don was very sick last year. _____ his long illness, he missed two months of school.

2. Maria didn't speak English when she came to the United States. _____, she didn't understand anyone, but gradually, she learned to communicate very well.

3. Last year, Monica _____ to change her job because she wasn't happy at work.

4. Doctors do not have a _____ for the common cold, but they do for many serious diseases.

assisted *(v.)*	careful *(adj.)*	for example	process *(n.)*

5. Alexandra is always very _____ when she walks across the street. She looks in both directions for cars.

6. Sending a text message is a simple _____.

7. The nurse _____ the doctor during the child's medical exam.

8. Modern pharmacies sell many different products in addition to medicine. _____, they sell magazines, candy, toys, and cards.

caused *(v.)*	curious *(adj.)*	in fact

9. Our college basketball team is very good. _____, the team lost only one game last year.

10. Cats are very _____ animals. They are interested in looking at everything.

11. Last winter, the ice on the roads _____ many car accidents.

Reading Skill

Understanding Coordinating Conjunctions

The coordinating conjunctions *and, but,* and *so* are important words. They help you understand the connection between ideas in a sentence. *And* connects two similar ideas or adds information. *But* connects two contrasting, or opposite, ideas. *So* connects a cause with an effect. Read the examples:

*Pasteur studied germs **and** learned how they cause diseases in animals and people.*

*Young Louis Pasteur enjoyed watching the chemist as he worked **and** listening to him assist the customers who came to him each day.*

*His doctor tried to help him, **but** there was no cure for rabies at that time.*

*He was especially interested in medicine, **so** he spent many hours every day with the chemist who lived in his small town.*

Read the sentences below. Complete each sentence with *and, but,* or *so*.

1. John studied very hard, _____ he passed the exam easily.

2. We cleaned every room in our house, _____ we washed all our dirty clothes.

3. I tried to sleep, _____ there was too much noise outside.

4. Vincent plays the piano, _____ he also plays the drums.

5. Barbara read this book last week, _____ she doesn't remember what the story is about.

6. I don't have any money, _____ I can't go with you to the movies tonight.

Topics for Discussion and Writing

1. When Louis Pasteur was a child, he was always interested in medicine. What subject were you interested in when you were a child? Are you still interested in that subject today? Write about this and explain your answer.

2. Many medical discoveries will be made in the future. What do you think will be the most important cure? Why? Discuss your ideas with your classmates. Decide which cures are the most important. Give your reasons.

3. Write in your journal. Think of a time when you or someone you know was not well. Describe the situation. What treatment helped this person? How did it help?

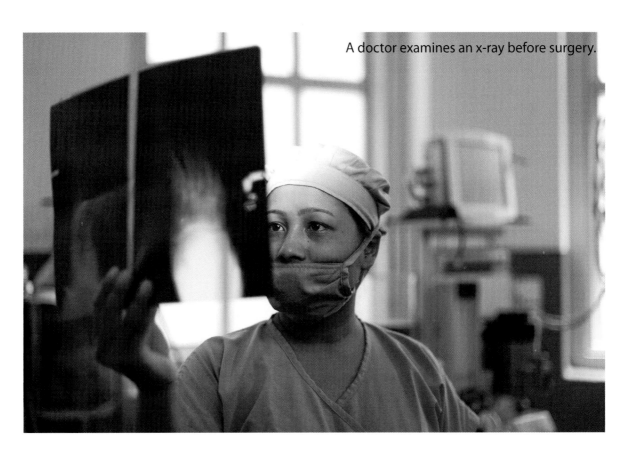

A doctor examines an x-ray before surgery.

Critical Thinking

1. Louis Pasteur's discovery of a rabies vaccine saved many lives. What other discoveries help to save lives today? Work in small groups and discuss your ideas. Then complete the chart below. When you are finished, compare your chart with other groups' charts. As a class, discuss these discoveries. Decide which discovery is the most important one.

Discoveries	Illnesses Cured
rabies vaccine	rabies

2. Pasteur developed the process of pasteurization over 100 years ago to make milk safe to drink. Today we know many other ways to prevent food from spoiling. Work with one or two classmates. Talk about some of these ways. Make a list and compare it with your other classmates' lists. Discuss which way is the most important, and why.

3. Discuss these questions with a partner. What medical discoveries of the past do you think are the most important? Why are these discoveries so important? How do they help people?

Cloze Quiz

Read the following passage. Fill in the blanks with the correct words from the list. Use each word or phrase only once.

became	carefully	school	thoughtful
but	learner	scientist	

As a schoolboy, Pasteur always worked slowly and _____(1)_____. At first, his teachers thought that young Louis might be a slow _____(2)_____. Through elementary school, high _____(3)_____, and college, Pasteur worked the same _____(4)_____ way. In fact, he was not a slow learner, _____(5)_____ a very intelligent young man. He _____(6)_____ a college professor and a _____(7)_____, and he continued to work very carefully.

age	devised	during	studied
benefit	diseases	prevent	such as

_____(8)_____ his lifetime, Pasteur _____(9)_____ germs and learned how they cause _____(10)_____ in animals and people. He developed vaccinations that _____(11)_____ many of these illnesses. He also _____(12)_____ the process of pasteurization, which stops food _____(13)_____ milk from spoiling. Louis Pasteur died on September 28, 1895, at the _____(14)_____ of 72. Modern medicine continues to _____(15)_____ from the work of this great scientist.

Crossword Puzzle

Review the words in the box below. Then read the clues on the next page. Write the words in the correct spaces in the puzzle.

assist	deadly	lifetime	process
benefit	devise	medicine	rabies
careful	disease	pharmacist	so
cure	especially	prevent	spoil
curious	inoculation		

Crossword Puzzle Clues

ACROSS CLUES

3. Pasteur worked slowly and paid attention. He was a very _____ man.

6. Pasteur liked to _____, or help, the druggist.

8. A _____ is a druggist.

10. Vaccinations help _____ many kinds of illnesses.

12. _____ is a very serious illness. We can get it from an animal bite.

14. Pasteur invented the _____ that helps keep milk drinkable.

15. A _____ is an illness.

16. Vaccinations are important for everyone, _____ for children.

18. We protect ourselves against some illnesses with an _____, or shot.

DOWN CLUES

1. Pasteur was the first person to _____, or invent, a way to keep milk from going bad.

2. Louis Pasteur discovered the _____ for rabies. His vaccination saved many people's lives.

4. The entire length of your life is called your _____.

5. Some diseases kill people. These are _____ diseases.

7. Germs cause milk to _____.

9. People who want to know all about many things are very _____.

11. We sometimes take _____ when we are sick.

13. We all _____ from medical discoveries.

17. Joseph Meister was dying, _____ Pasteur vaccinated him even though he wasn't sure it would work.

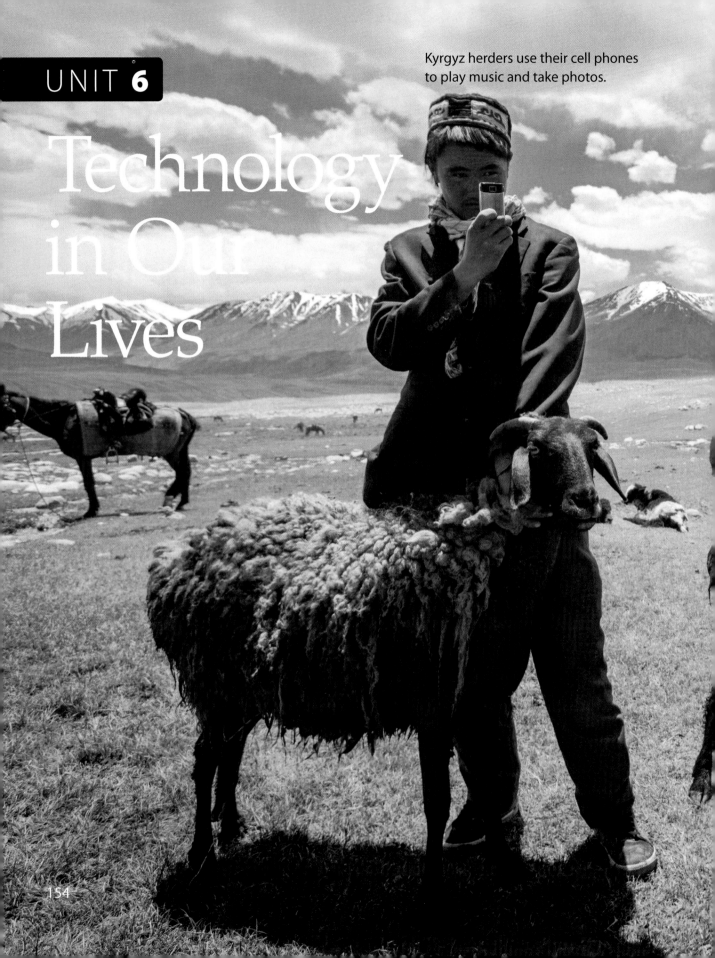

UNIT 6

Technology in Our Lives

Kyrgyz herders use their cell phones to play music and take photos.

154

1. What kinds of technology do you use every day?

2. How can technology be helpful? How can technology cause problems?

155

CHAPTER **11** The Cell Phone Debate

Tourists take photos with their cell phones.

Prereading

1. Read the title of this chapter. Why do people have debates?
   a. They have different opinions.
   b. They have the same opinion.
   c. They have a lot of questions.

2. Where can you use your cell phone? Where can't you use your cell phone? Ask your classmates and write their answers on the chart. Discuss your answers.

Where can you use your cell phone?	Where can't you use your cell phone?

Reading

Read each paragraph carefully. Then answer the questions.

The Cell Phone Debate

The United States has 58 national parks. Millions of people from all over the country and around the world visit these parks every year. They come for many different reasons, for example, to climb mountains, walk along the endless trails, or bike on the many scenic paths. All the visitors come to the parks to enjoy nature's beauty, breathe the fresh air, and listen to the sounds of the birds. But some visitors also hear the ringing of cell phones, and they are not happy about that.

1. The United States has 58 **national** parks. **National** refers to
   a. a city.
   b. a state.
   c. a country.

2. They come for many different reasons, for example, to **climb** mountains, walk along the **endless trails**, or bike on the many scenic paths.
   a. **Climb** means
      1. to go up.
      2. to look at.
      3. to find.
   b. **Endless** means very
      1. beautiful.
      2. long.
      3. old.
   c. A **trail** is
      1. a path.
      2. a sidewalk.
      3. a highway.

3. **But some visitors also hear the ringing of cell phones, and they are not happy about that.**
   The visitors are not happy because
   a. they don't like the parks.
   b. they can't use their cell phones.
   c. they don't like to hear the sounds of cell phones.

Yellowstone National Park is one of the largest national parks in the United States. It is in the northwest part of the country. Cell phone service is available in some parts of Yellowstone. Charles Yoo, a visitor to the park, thinks this is very useful. "I believe cell phone service is important in the park. It can be very helpful if a visitor is sick or injured." Many people agree with Charles. They think that it's useful to have a cell phone in the park. Amber Rodriquez, another park visitor, says, "Cell phones can help me to find directions and look up information about the plants and wildlife in the park, too. I can also share photos of the park on social media, such as Facebook and Twitter. This makes my trip more exciting."

4. **Cell phone service is available in some parts of Yellowstone.**
   This means
   a. you can never make or receive phone calls in Yellowstone.
   b. you can sometimes make and receive phone calls in Yellowstone.
   c. you can always make and receive phone calls in Yellowstone.

5. An **injured** person is
   a. hurt.
   b. lost.
   c. sick.

6. When you **agree with** someone,
   a. you have a different opinion.
   b. you have the same opinion.

7. **Wildlife** is
   a. flowers.
   b. trees.
   c. animals.

8. **Share** photos means
   a. to show photos to other people.
   b. to sell photos to other people.
   c. to take photos of other people.

9. What are examples of **social media**? Check (√) all that apply.
   a. _____ Television
   b. _____ Twitter
   c. _____ Radio
   d. _____ Facebook
   e. _____ Telephone
   f. _____ Blogs
   g. _____ Instagram

10. What do you think the next paragraph will discuss?
    a. People who do not want cell phone service in national parks
    b. People who want cell phone service in national parks
    c. The reasons why people visit national parks

However, some people disagree with Charles and Amber. They believe that cell phones do not belong in national parks. "Can you imagine looking at a peaceful lake and hearing the sound of a person shouting into his cell phone? I prefer to hear the sounds of the birds singing than to hear the ringing of a cell phone," argues Steven Padilla. "I use technology all the time in my daily life. I come to Yellowstone every year to get away from it. I love the peace and quiet here."

11. When you **disagree with** someone,
    a. you have a different opinion.
    b. you have the same opinion.

12. **Some people believe that cell phones do not belong in national parks.**
    These people believe that
    a. cell phones are useful in national parks.
    b. people shouldn't use cell phones in national parks.
    c. cell phones can be exciting in national parks.

13. You **argue** about something because
    a. you agree with someone.
    b. you don't understand someone.
    c. you disagree with someone.

14. Steven Padilla says, "**I come to Yellowstone every year to get away from it.**"
This means he wants to
   a. take a break from technology.
   b. leave Yellowstone.
   c. use his cell phone in Yellowstone.

Al Nash works at Yellowstone National Park. "Technology is a challenge for all of us at the park. Our job is to give visitors enjoyment. We need to allow them to get away from the hustle and bustle of their lives. At the same time, we need to keep people safe. People can get help quickly with cell phones." Right now, cell phone service is available only in some parts of the park. That may change soon as more and more people depend on technology for almost every part of their daily lives.

15. When you have a **challenge,** you have
   a. a problem to take care of.
   b. a question to ask.
   c. a place to visit.

16. We need to **allow** visitors to get away from the **hustle and bustle of their daily lives.**
   a. **Allow** means
      1. tell.
      2. let.
      3. ask.
   b. The **hustle and bustle of their daily lives** means
      1. all of their problems.
      2. their difficult jobs.
      3. their busy and noisy activities every day.

17. When you **depend on** something, you
   a. like it.
   b. need it.
   c. want it.

A woman talks on a cell phone at the Grand Canyon.

🎧 **Read the complete passage. Then answer the questions that follow.**

CD 1
TR 12

The Cell Phone Debate

1   The United States has 58 national parks. Millions of people from all over the
2 country and around the world visit these parks every year. They come for many
3 different reasons, for example, to climb mountains, walk along the endless trails, or
4 bike on the many scenic paths. All the visitors come to the parks to enjoy nature's
5 beauty, breathe the fresh air, and listen to the sounds of the birds. But some visitors
6 also hear the ringing of cell phones, and they are not happy about that.
7   Yellowstone National Park is one of the largest national parks in the United States.
8 It is in the northwest part of the country. Cell phone service is available in some parts
9 of Yellowstone. Charles Yoo, a visitor to the park, thinks this is very useful. "I believe
10 cell phone service is important in the park. It can be very helpful if a visitor is sick or
11 injured." Many people agree with Charles. They think that it's useful to have a cell
12 phone in the park. Amber Rodriquez, another park visitor, says, "Cell phones can
13 help me to find directions and look up information about the plants and wildlife in
14 the park, too. I can also share photos of the park on social media, such as Facebook
15 and Twitter. This makes my trip more exciting."
16   However, some people disagree with Charles and Amber. They believe that cell
17 phones do not belong in national parks. "Can you imagine looking at a peaceful lake

18 and hearing the sound of a person shouting into his cell phone? I prefer to hear the
19 sounds of the birds singing than to hear the ringing of a cell phone," argues Steven
20 Padilla. "I use technology all the time in my daily life. I come to Yellowstone every
21 year to get away from it. I love the peace and quiet here."

22   Al Nash works at Yellowstone National Park. "Technology is a challenge for all of
23 us at the park. Our job is to give visitors enjoyment. We need to allow them to get
24 away from the hustle and bustle of their lives. At the same time, we need to keep
25 people safe. People can get help quickly with cell phones." Right now, cell phone
26 service is available only in some parts of the park. That may change soon as more and
27 more people depend on technology for almost every part of their daily lives.

Scanning for Information

**Read the questions. Then go back to the complete passage and scan quickly for the answers.
Check (√) or circle the letter of the correct answers.**

1. Why do so many people visit national parks in the United States? Check (√) all that apply.
   a. _____ To grow flowers and trees
   b. _____ To climb mountains
   c. _____ To hunt wildlife
   d. _____ To bike on scenic paths
   e. _____ To help people who are lost
   f. _____ To walk along the trails
   g. _____ To work in the parks
   h. _____ To relax and enjoy nature

2. How can a cell phone be useful in a national park? Check (√) all that apply.
   a. _____ People can call for help if they are hurt.
   b. _____ People can take photos with a cell phone.
   c. _____ People can use cells phones by a lake.
   d. _____ People can get directions with their cell phones.
   e. _____ Cell phones ring loudly so people can hear them.
   f. _____ People can charge their cell phone battery.

3. Why do some people dislike cell phones in national parks? Check (√) all that apply.
   a. _____ Because cell phones ring loudly
   b. _____ Because people take photos with them
   c. _____ Because some people do not like technology
   d. _____ Because some people shout into their cell phones
   e. _____ Because many people prefer peace and quiet in the park

4. Which people agree with using cell phones in national parks? Check (√) all that apply.

    a. _____ Steven Padilla

    b. _____ Al Nash

    c. _____ Amber Rodriquez

    d. _____ Charles Yoo

5. _____ True _____ False   Cell phone service is available now in all parts of Yellowstone National Park.

6. _____ True _____ False   Cell phone service may be available soon in all parts of Yellowstone National Park.

7. What is the main idea of this passage?

    a. Everyone thinks cell phone service in national parks is a bad idea.

    b. Cell phone service will soon be available in all national parks.

    c. People do not agree that cell phone service in national parks is a good idea.

Vocabulary Skill

Recognizing Word Forms

In English, some verbs *(v.)* can become nouns *(n.)* by adding the suffix *-ment,* for example, *agree (v.), agreement (n.).*

Read the sentences below. Decide if the correct word is a noun or a verb. Circle your answer. Do the examples below as a class before you begin.

    EXAMPLES:

    a. Many people agree / agreement that cell phones are useful.
             (v.)   *(n.)*

    b. Not everyone is in agree / agreement about using cell phones in the park.
                 (v.)   *(n.)*

1. Visitors argue / argument that cell phones are a good idea in Yellowstone National Park.
         (v.)   *(n.)*

2. This is an important argue / argument in many national parks.
               (v.)   *(n.)*

3. People disagree / disagreement about using technology on vacation.
        (v.)   *(n.)*

4. There is a disagree / disagreement about the importance of cell phone service in this very
         (v.)   *(n.)*
peaceful place.

5. Millions of people get a lot of <u>enjoy / enjoyment</u> from visiting national parks.
                                               (v.)   *(n.)*

6. They <u>enjoy / enjoyment</u> the beauty and quiet of Yellowstone.
        (v.)   *(n.)*

7. Some people feel a lot of <u>excite / excitement</u> about mountain climbing.
                                  (v.)   *(n.)*

8. Mountain climbing <u>excites / excitement</u> many visitors.
                      (v.)   *(n.)*

Vocabulary in Context

Read the following sentences. Choose the correct word or phrase for each sentence. Fill in the blanks.

argue *(v.)*	share *(v.)*	wildlife *(n.)*

1. My friends and I _____ photos of our vacations on Facebook and Instagram.

2. The students enjoy the _____ on the beautiful campus. They love to watch the birds and the squirrels.

3. Silvana and Jessica are roommates. They sometimes _____ about cleaning their apartment. Silvana is very neat, but Jessica is not.

allow *(v.)*	depend *(v.)*	trail *(n.)*

4. Hernando enjoys walking along the _____ in the park after class.

5. Our teacher doesn't _____ us to use cell phones. We have to put them away when we get to class.

6. Many people _____ on the Internet to communicate with their families in other countries.

challenge *(n.)*	debate *(n.)*	disagree *(v.)*	injured *(adj.)*

7. It can be a _____ to learn a new language, but it is not impossible.

8. Can you give me your seat? I am _____ and I need to sit down.

9. Sophia and Grace _____ about a new color for their kitchen. Sophia wants to paint it green, but Grace wants to paint it yellow.

10. Parents often have a _____ about giving cell phones to their children. They often disagree on the best age for children to have cell phones.

Reading Skill

Using a For and Against Chart

For and Against Charts show the arguments for both sides of a debate in a clear way. It is important to know how to create and use a For and Against Chart. These charts help you understand both sides of a debate or issue from a reading passage.

Read the passage again. Write the information in the chart below.

The Cell Phone Debate	
Arguments *For* Allowing Cell Phones in National Parks	Arguments *Against* Allowing Cell Phones in National Parks
-They help people find directions.	-People shout into their cell phones.

Topics for Discussion and Writing

1. What are some other arguments for not allowing cell phones in national parks?

2. What are some other arguments for allowing cell phones in national parks?

3. Write in your journal. Do you think that cell phones belong in national parks? Why or why not?

Critical Thinking

1. There are many places where people do not want cell phones, for example, in classrooms and libraries. Work in a small group. Decide where cell phones belong and where they do not belong. Compare your answers with the rest of the class.

2. Is it a good idea for students to use cell phones in class? Divide your class into two groups. One group will discuss arguments for cell phones in class. The other group will discuss arguments against cell phones in class. Each group will write their argument in the chart below and then have a class debate.

Debate: Using Cell Phones in Class	
Group 1: Arguments *For* Using Cell Phones in Class	Group 2: Arguments *Against* Using Cell Phones in Class

3. Work with a partner. Some people want to use their cell phones in national parks. Other people think it is a bad idea. Write some rules for using cell phones in national parks that will make most people happy.

Cloze Quiz

Read the following passage. Fill in the blanks with the correct words from the list. Use each word or phrase only once.

agree	service	social media	visitor
injured	share	trip	wildlife

Yellowstone National Park is one of the largest national parks in the United States.

It is in the northwest part of the country. Cell phone _____ is available
(1)

in some parts of Yellowstone. Charles Yoo, a visitor to the park, thinks this is very useful. "I believe cell phone service is important in the park. It can be very helpful if a visitor is sick or _____(2)_____." Many people _____(3)_____ with Charles. They think that it's useful to have a cell phone in the park. Amber Rodriquez, another park _____(4)_____, says, "Cell phones can help me to find directions and give me information about the plants and _____(5)_____ in the park, too. I can also _____(6)_____ photos of the park on _____(7)_____, such as Facebook and Twitter. This makes my _____(8)_____ more exciting."

allow	belong	disagree	sound
argues	challenge	quiet	

However, some people _____(9)_____ with Charles and Amber. They believe that cell phones do not _____(10)_____ in national parks. "Can you imagine looking at a peaceful lake and hearing the _____(11)_____ of a person shouting into his cell phone? I prefer to hear the sounds of the birds singing than to hear the ringing of a cell phone,"_____(12)_____ Steven Padilla. "I use technology all the time in my daily life. I come to Yellowstone every year to get away from it. I love the peace and _____(13)_____ here."

Al Nash works at Yellowstone National Park. "Technology is a _____(14)_____ for all of us at the park. Our job is to give visitors enjoyment. We need to _____(15)_____ them to get away from the hustle and bustle of their daily lives.

Crossword Puzzle

Review the words in the box below. Then read the clues on the next page. Write the words in the correct spaces in the puzzle.

agree	challenge	enjoy	service
allow	debate	excitement	share
argue	depend	injured	trail
belong	disagree	national	

Crossword Puzzle Clues

ACROSS CLUES

4. There is no Internet _____ in this building.

6. The teacher does not _____ students to use cell phones in her class.

7. A path is also called a _____.

8. You have a _____ when you have different points of view on a subject.

10. We all _____ on electricity for many things in our lives.

13. When someone is _____, he or she is hurt.

14. The United States has many parks. Some are city parks, some are state parks, and some are _____ parks.

15. I _____ with you. I have the same opinion as you do.

DOWN CLUES

1. Dogs do not _____ in a food store. You must keep them outside.

2. We _____ with you. We think differently on this subject.

3. Stairs are a _____ for some people with health problems.

5. When children see wild animals in a park, they feel a lot of _____!

9. When you _____ with someone, you express a different opinion.

11. Did you forget your textbook? I can _____ my book with you today.

12. People _____ being out in the fresh air of a national park.

CHAPTER 12

Clues and Criminal Investigation

An investigator looks at fingerprints.

Prereading

1. Police look for clues to help solve a crime. Work with a partner. Look at the list of clues in the chart below. What type of crime can these clues help solve? Some clues may help solve more than one kind of crime. When you are finished, compare your work with your other classmates' work.

Clues	Types of Crime
blood	
bullets	
clothing	
dirt	
fingerprints	
footprints	
hair	
pieces of glass	
a ransom note	

2. Think of a crime that you heard about or read about. Describe it to your partner. What clues did the police use to help them solve this crime?

3. Read the title of this passage. What do you think the reading will be about?

Reading

Read each paragraph carefully. Then answer the questions.

Clues and Criminal Investigation

Imagine that you want to solve a crime, such as a robbery or a murder. How do you start? What types of evidence do you look for? Crime experts all have a basic principle, or belief: A criminal always brings something to the scene of a crime and always leaves something there. As a result, crime experts always begin their criminal investigation with a careful examination of the crime scene. The crime scene is the place where the crime occurred.

1. A **crime expert** is
   a. a professional at committing crimes.
   b. a professional at solving crimes.

2. A **principle** is
   a. an idea that you have.
   b. evidence that you have.
   c. a belief that you have.

3. What do crime experts think?
   a. They think that they will always find clues at the scene of a crime.
   b. They think that they can solve every crime that occurs.
   c. They think that criminals are usually not very careful.

4. What do you think the next paragraph will discuss?
   a. How the police catch criminals
   b. What happens at the crime scene
   c. How many types of crimes there are

When criminal investigators arrive at the crime scene, they look for evidence, or clues, from the criminal. This evidence includes footprints, fingerprints, lip prints on glasses, hair, blood, clothing fibers, and bullet shells, for example. These are all clues that criminals often leave behind. Investigators take some clues to laboratories and analyze them. For instance, they "lift," or take, fingerprints from a glass, a door, or a table. They use computers to compare the fingerprints with the millions of fingerprints on file with the police, the Federal Bureau of Investigation (FBI), and other agencies.

5. A **crime scene** is
   a. a part of a movie.
   b. the place where the crime occurred.
   c. a description of the crime.

6. **Evidence** means
   a. clues.
   b. criminals.
   c. beliefs.

7. Some examples of clues are

   _____.

8. Investigators take some clues to laboratories and **analyze** them. For instance, they "**lift**," or take, fingerprints from a glass, a door, or a table.
   a. **Analyze** means
      1. take something to a laboratory.
      2. study something carefully.
      3. give something to an investigator.
   b. **Lift** means
      1. find.
      2. take.
      3. examine.

9. What do you think the next paragraphs will discuss?
   a. How the police find criminals
   b. How the FBI helps solve crimes
   c. How experts examine the evidence

In the case of murder, experts examine blood. Then they compare it to the blood of the victim. If the blood isn't the victim's, then it might be the murderer's. Furthermore, experts can examine the DNA from a person's cells, such as skin cells or blood cells. Like fingerprints, each person's DNA is unique. This means that everyone's DNA is different. All these clues help find the criminal.

In some cases, criminals use a gun during a crime. Every gun leaves distinctive marks on a bullet. The police may find a bullet at the scene or recover a bullet from a victim's body. Experts can examine the marks on the bullet. They can prove that it came from a specific gun. This clue is strong evidence that the owner of the gun may be guilty. Consequently, the police will suspect that this person committed the crime.

10. A **victim** is
   a. the person who committed the crime.
   b. the person who is harmed in a crime.

11. **Furthermore** means
   a. in addition.
   b. farther away.
   c. however.

12. Like fingerprints, each person's DNA is **unique,** which means that everyone's DNA is different.
   a. **Unique** means
      1. from a person's body.
      2. original or individual.
      3. a special clue.
   b. Which one of the following sentences is true?
      1. Each person's DNA and fingerprints are different from every other person's.
      2. Each person's DNA is different from every other person's, but his or her fingerprints are not.
      3. Each person's fingerprints are different from every other person's, but their DNA is not.

13. Every gun leaves **distinctive** marks on a bullet.
   a. **Distinctive** means
      1. particular.
      2. clear.
      3. metal.
   b. The markings on bullets from two different guns
      1. can sometimes be the same.
      2. can never be the same.

14. A gun's **owner** is
    a. the person who used the gun.
    b. the person that the gun belongs to.
    c. the person who found the gun.

15. **The police suspect that this person committed a crime.**
    a. This sentence means that
       1. the police are sure that a specific person committed a crime.
       2. the police believe that a specific person committed a crime.
    b. **Suspect** means
       1. think that something is true.
       2. know that something is true.

16. **Consequently** means
    a. in addition.
    b. however.
    c. as a result.

Clues from the scene of a crime help the police identify a suspect. If other evidence supports these clues, then police can charge the suspect with the crime. It is important to remember, however, that in the United States, a person is innocent until a court proves that he or she is guilty.

17. The police charge a suspect with a crime when
    a. they find a gun that belongs to that person.
    b. they have blood and bullets from the scene of the crime.
    c. they have evidence to show that maybe the person committed the crime.

18. a. The words **innocent** and **guilty**
       1. have the opposite meanings.
       2. have the same meaning.
    b. An **innocent** person
       1. committed a crime.
       2. did not commit a crime.
    c. A **guilty** person
       1. committed a crime.
       2. did not commit a crime.

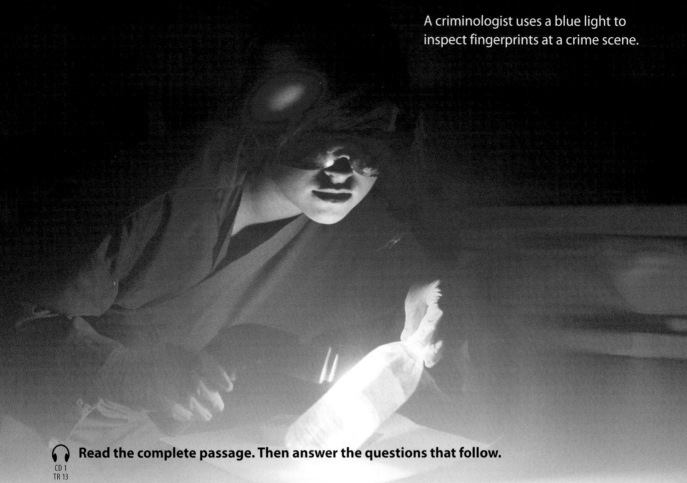

A criminologist uses a blue light to inspect fingerprints at a crime scene.

🎧 **Read the complete passage. Then answer the questions that follow.**

CD 1
TR 13

Clues and Criminal Investigation

1   Imagine that you want to solve a crime, such as a robbery or a murder. How do
2 you start? What types of evidence do you look for? Crime experts all have a basic
3 principle, or belief: A criminal always brings something to the scene of a crime and
4 always leaves something there. As a result, crime experts always begin their criminal
5 investigation with a careful examination of the crime scene. The crime scene is the
6 place where the crime occurred.

7   When criminal investigators arrive at the crime scene, they look for evidence, or
8 clues, from the criminal. This evidence includes footprints, fingerprints, lip prints
9 on glasses, hair, blood, clothing fibers, and bullet shells, for example. These are all
10 clues that criminals often leave behind. Investigators take some clues to laboratories
11 and analyze them. For instance, they "lift," or take, fingerprints from a glass, a door,
12 or a table. They use computers to compare the fingerprints with the millions of
13 fingerprints on file with the police, the Federal Bureau of Investigation (FBI), and
14 other agencies.

15   In the case of murder, experts examine blood. Then they compare it to the
16 blood of the victim. If the blood isn't the victim's, then it might be the murderer's.
17 Furthermore, experts can examine the DNA from a person's cells, such as skin cells
18 or blood cells. Like fingerprints, each person's DNA is unique. This means that
19 everyone's DNA is different. All these clues help find the criminal.

20   In some cases, criminals use a gun during a crime. Every gun leaves distinctive
21 marks on a bullet. The police may find a bullet at the scene or recover a bullet from
22 a victim's body. Experts can examine the marks on the bullet. They can prove that it
23 came from a specific gun. This clue is strong evidence that the owner of the gun may
24 be guilty. Consequently, the police will suspect that this person committed the crime.

25   Clues from the scene of a crime help the police identify a suspect. If other evidence
26 supports these clues, then police can charge the suspect with the crime. It is important
27 to remember, however, that in the United States, a person is innocent until a court
28 proves that he or she is guilty.

Scanning for Information

Read the questions. Then go back to the complete passage and scan quickly for the answers. Circle the letter of the correct answer or write your answer in the space provided.

1. What do all crime experts believe?

_____

_____

2. Why are fingerprints from the scene of a crime compared with the fingerprints on file with the police, the FBI, and other agencies?

_____

_____

3. If the blood found at the scene of a murder isn't the victim's blood, why might it be the murderer's blood?

_____

4. Why are blood, skin, and fingerprints so important to crime experts?

_____

5. What is the main idea of this story?
   a. Criminals often leave many clues at the scene of a crime.
   b. Fingerprints and bullets are important evidence of crimes.
   c. Crime experts find and analyze a variety of clues to identify criminals.

Vocabulary Skill

Recognizing Word Forms

In English, some nouns (n.) become adjectives (adj.) by adding -ful, for example, use (n.), useful (adj.).

Read the sentences below. Decide if the correct word is a noun or an adjective. Circle your answer. Do the examples below as a class before you begin.

EXAMPLES:

a. Investigators <u>use / useful</u> computers to compare fingerprints.
   (n.)   (adj.)

b. Computers are <u>use / useful</u> for analyzing evidence.
   (n.)   (adj.)

1. Criminal investigators are very <u>skill / skillful</u>.
   (n.)   (adj.)

2. Their <u>skill / skillful</u> is very important in helping them solve crimes.
   (n.)   (adj.)

3. Investigators are often <u>success / successful</u> in solving crimes.
   (n.)   (adj.)

4. Their <u>success / successful</u> usually depends on the evidence.
   (n.)   (adj.)

5. The police need <u>help / helpful</u> to find the criminal.
   (n.)   (adj.)

6. DNA evidence is very <u>help / helpful</u> to the police.
   (n.)   (adj.)

7. Investigators are <u>care / careful</u> when they look for clues.
   (n.)   (adj.)

8. They take a lot of <u>care / careful</u> when they "lift" fingerprints.
   (n.)   (adj.)

Vocabulary in Context

Read the following sentences. Choose the correct word or phrase for each sentence. Fill in the blanks.

| expert *(n.)* | principle *(n.)* | suspects *(v.)* |

1. Jake _____ that he is getting a new bicycle for his birthday. He heard his parents talking about it.

2. Dr. Lim is an animal doctor. He is a(n) _____ on illnesses in most pets.

3. A strong _____ in the United States is that all people are equal.

| consequently *(adv.)* | evidence *(n.)* | if *(conj.)* |

4. I think Marty dropped my cell phone and broke it. I don't have any _____, so I cannot prove it.

5. I am busy right now, so I can't help you. I will help you later _____ I have enough time.

6. Jennifer goes to class every day and does her homework every night. She has a part-time job on weekends. _____, Jennifer doesn't have a lot of free time.

| furthermore *(adv.)* | investigate *(v.)* | occurred *(v.)* |

7. Tom is a very busy person. He works every day from 9 a.m. to 7 p.m. and takes care of his children at night. _____, he attends college classes on the weekends.

8. Linda heard a strange sound in her apartment. When she went to _____, she saw a mouse under the stairs!

9. A huge snowstorm _____ yesterday in this city, so the schools will be closed until next week.

Reading Skill

Understanding Chronological Order

It is important to understand the order in which events occur. This is called chronological order. Some events take place before or after other events occur. For example:

Someone robs a bank. The police come to the bank. They look for clues.

Read the list of actions below. Write them in the correct order in which they logically occur.

- Investigators look for evidence at the crime scene.
- The investigators take the fingerprints to laboratories and analyze them.
- Criminal investigators arrive at the crime scene.
- They use computers to compare the fingerprints with fingerprints on file with the police, the FBI, and other agencies.
- ~~Investigators find fingerprints at the crime scene.~~
- If the fingerprints match with fingerprints on file, the police can identify a suspect.
- ~~Someone commits a crime.~~

1. *Someone commits a crime.* _____

2. _____

3. _____

4. *Investigators find fingerprints at the crime scene.* _____

5. _____

6. _____

7. _____

Topics for Discussion and Writing

1. Work with two or three classmates. Find a description of a crime in a book, magazine, or newspaper. Read the description of the crime, the clues, and the suspect. Decide if the suspect is guilty or innocent. Write a paragraph describing your decision. Each group will present their ideas to the class. Do your classmates agree with each group's decision?

2. Many people enjoy watching TV programs and movies and reading books about crimes and criminal investigations. Do you enjoy watching these kinds of shows or books? Why or why not? Why do you think these shows and books are popular? Discuss your reasons with your classmates.

3. What do you think is the most important kind of evidence at a crime scene? Why is this evidence the most important? Explain your opinion.

4. Write in your journal. Think about a crime you read about. Describe the crime. What happened? When and where did this crime take place? How did the police investigate it? What clues did they find? How did they solve the crime? Share your story with a classmate. Which crime was more difficult to solve? Why?

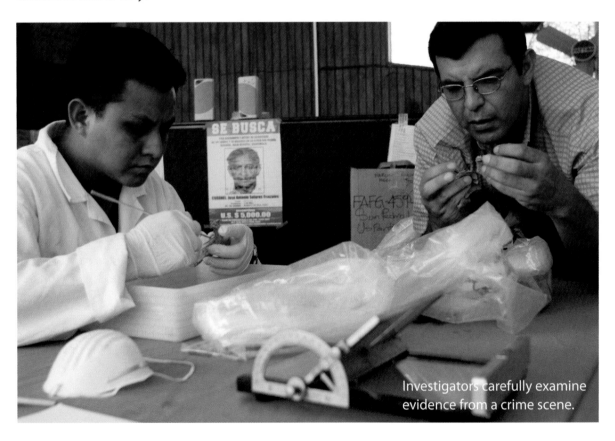

Investigators carefully examine evidence from a crime scene.

Critical Thinking

1. Work with two or three classmates. Imagine that you are a group of crime experts. The police asked you to investigate the following crimes. What clues will you look for at the scene of each crime? What additional evidence will you try to get in order to identify a suspect for each of these crimes? Write your ideas in the chart below.

Type of Crime	Clues at the Scene of the Crime	Additional Evidence
a murder		
a kidnapping		
a house break-in		
a jewelry store robbery		

2. Work with one or two classmates. Invent a crime and write a list of some evidence to leave at the scene of the crime. Then have your classmates investigate your crime and try to solve it. When you are finished, discuss your evidence. Which group had the best clues?

3. Discuss these questions with a partner. In the United States, a person is innocent until the court proves that he or she is guilty. Do you think this idea is important in law? Why or why not? Give reasons.

Cloze Quiz

Read the following passage. Fill in the blanks with the correct words from the list. Use each word only once.

belief	case	evidence	investigators	occurred
careful	crime	furthermore	leaves	result

Imagine that you want to solve a _____ (1), such as a robbery or a murder. How do you start? What types of _____ (2) do you look for? Crime experts all have a basic principle, or _____ (3): A criminal always brings something to the scene of a crime and always _____ (4) something there. As a _____ (5), crime experts always begin their criminal investigation with a _____ (6) examination of the crime scene. The crime scene is the place where the crime _____ (7).

When criminal _____ (8) arrive at the crime scene, they look for evidence, or clues, from the criminal. This evidence includes footprints, fingerprints, lip prints on glasses, hair, blood, clothing fibers, and bullet shells, for example. In the _____ (9) of murder, experts examine blood. Then they compare it to the blood of the victim. If the blood isn't the victim's, then it might be the murderer's. _____ (10), experts can examine the DNA from a person's cells, such as skin cells or blood cells. Like fingerprints, each person's DNA is unique. This means that everyone's DNA is different. All these clues help to find the criminal.

| bullet | consequently | guilty | owner | specific |
| clues | experts | gun | scene | suspect |

In some cases, criminals use a gun during a crime. Every _____ (11)

leaves distinctive marks on a _____ (12). The police may find a

bullet at the _____ (13) or recover a bullet from a victim's body.

_____ (14) can examine the marks on the bullet. They can prove that

it came from a _____ (15) gun. This clue is strong evidence that the

_____ (16) of the gun may be guilty. _____ (17),

the police will _____ (18) that this person committed the crime.

_____ (19) from the scene of a crime help the police identify a suspect.

If other evidence supports these clues, then police can charge the suspect with the

crime. It is important to remember, however, that in the United States, a person is

innocent until a court proves that he or she is _____ (20).

Crossword Puzzle

Review the words in the box below. Then read the clues on the next page. Write the words in the correct spaces in the puzzle.

bullet	example	innocent	solve
crimes	experts	occur	suspect
distinctive	fingerprints	owner	unique
DNA	guilty	principle	victim
evidence			

Crossword Puzzle Clues

ACROSS CLUES

2. Murder, robbery, kidnapping, and car theft are all serious _____.

7. John was the _____ of a robbery yesterday. Someone went up to him on the street and stole his wallet.

8. I am the _____ of this house. It belongs to me.

10. The police don't have any _____, or clues, in this case yet.

11. Everyone's fingerprints are _____. No two people have the same fingerprints.

13. The police may ask many different _____ for help to solve a crime: chemists, dentists, doctors, etc.

14. Many specialists help the police _____ crimes.

16. Mary did not steal John's wallet. She is _____ of that crime.

17. The police _____ that the robber entered the victim's apartment through a window. The window in the kitchen was open.

DOWN CLUES

1. I have a very simple _____, or belief: I try my best with everything I do.

3. The police look for clues, for _____, blood, hair, and bullets.

4. Crimes _____, or take place, every day.

5. The lines on a person's fingers are called _____.

6. My dog has _____ markings. He has a black leg, a black ear, and a black spot on his head.

9. Rick is in prison now because he is _____ of robbing a bank.

12. A gun leaves particular markings on a _____.

15. Each person's _____ is particular to him or her, just like his or her fingerprints.

INDEX OF KEY WORDS AND PHRASES

Words with **AWL** beside them are on the Academic Word List (AWL), Coxhead (2000). The AWL is a list of the 570 highest-frequency academic word families that regularly appear in academic texts. Researcher Avril Coxhead compiled this list from a corpus of 3.5 million words.

SKILLS INDEX

C

CRITICAL THINKING
charts, 28, 44, 58, 74, 88, 104, 150, 166, 181
group activities, 15, 44, 58, 74, 88, 118, 134, 150, 166, 181
lists, 28, 58, 74, 88, 118, 134, 150, 181
partner activities, 15, 28, 44, 74, 88, 104, 118, 134, 150, 166, 181
schedules, 15

G

GRAMMAR AND USAGE
word forms
adjectives that become adverbs by adding -*ly*, 84–85
adjectives that become nouns by adding -*ness*, 101
nouns that become adjectives by adding -*ful*, 12, 177
verbs that become nouns by adding -*ence* or -*ance*, 131
verbs that become nouns by adding -*ment*, 114, 163–164
verbs that become nouns by adding -*tion*, 146–147
verbs that become nouns by dropping the final -*e* and adding -*tion*, 146–147
words that can be either nouns or verbs, 25–26, 41, 54–55, 71

L

LISTENING/SPEAKING
asking/answering questions, 104
discussion, 14, 27–28, 43, 57, 74, 87, 103, 117, 134, 149, 165, 180
interviewing, 134
partner activities, 18, 28, 44, 48, 74, 94, 103, 124
reporting, 28

R

READING
charts, 48, 102–103, 104, 156, 166
comprehension, 5–9, 19–23, 35–38, 49–52, 65–68, 79–82, 95–98, 109–111, 125–128, 139–143, 157–160, 171–174
descriptions, 124, 134, 182
lists, 18, 170
prereading, 4, 18–19, 34, 48, 64, 78, 94–95, 108, 124–125, 138–139, 156, 170–171
scanning for information, 11, 25, 40, 54, 70, 84, 100, 113, 130, 145–146, 162–163, 176–177
vocabulary in context, 13, 26–27, 42, 55–56, 72, 85–86, 102, 115, 132, 147–148, 164–165, 178

T

TEST-TAKING SKILLS
cloze quizzes, 15, 29, 45, 59, 75, 88–89, 105, 118–119, 135, 151, 166–167, 182–183
fill in blanks, 13, 26–27, 42, 55–56, 72, 85–86, 102, 115, 132, 147–148, 164–165, 178

multiple-choice questions, 5–9, 19–23, 25, 35–38, 40, 48, 49–52, 65–68, 70, 78, 79–82, 94, 95–98, 100, 109–111, 113, 124, 125–128, 138–143, 157–160, 171–174

putting items in order, 43, 179

short-answer questions, 19, 25, 35–36, 38, 40, 48, 50–51, 64, 84, 126–127, 141, 142, 172, 176

true/false questions, 7, 19, 22, 35, 37, 50–51, 65, 67, 95, 97–98, 109–111, 125–127, 141, 163

yes/no questions, 20, 70, 97, 139

TOPICS

the best place to live, 94–107

Cabey-Gray family, 34–47

the cell phone debate, 156–169

clues and criminal investigation, 170–185

healthy in college, 4–17

it's ok to make mistakes!, 64–77

learning a second language, 18–31

Louis Pasteur, 138–153

Margaret Mead, 124–137

McCaughey family, 48–61

the New York City Marathon, 108–121

super memory, 78–91

V

VISUAL LITERACY

photographs, 48, 83, 94

W

WRITING

charts, 18, 28, 44, 58, 74, 88, 94–95, 104, 150, 156, 165, 170, 181

crossword puzzles, 16–17, 30–31, 46–47, 60–61, 76–77, 90–91, 106–107, 120–121, 136–137, 152–153, 168–169, 184–185

descriptions, 124, 134, 149, 180

discussion, 134

examples, 27, 134

explanations, 28, 43, 57, 103, 134, 149, 180

group activities, 44, 58, 118, 150, 166, 181

journals, 14, 21–24, 27, 28, 43, 57, 74, 87, 103, 117, 134, 149, 180

letters, 27, 87, 117

lists, 14–15, 18, 28, 58, 74, 88, 103, 108, 118, 134, 150, 170, 181

paragraphs, 43, 57, 134, 180

partner activities, 18, 28, 44, 48, 74, 94, 103, 118, 124, 166, 170–171, 181

plans, 134

reasons, 58, 94, 103, 108, 180, 181

schedules, 15, 57

sentences, 124

NOTES

NOTES

NOTES

English Language Programs
Ohio Northern University
525 S. Main Street
Ada, OH 45810